Letters From
Maybe

True Life Letters From
An Imaginary Town

Revised

Michael Pearson

CSS Publishing Company, Inc., Lima, Ohio

LETTERS FROM MAYBE
REVISED

Some scripture quotations are from the New Revised Standard Version of the Bible, copyright 1989 by the Division of Christian Education of the National Council of the Churches of Christ in the USA. Used by permission.

Scripture quotations marked (CEV) are from the Contemporary English Version of the Holy Bible. Copyright © The American Bible Society 1995. Used by permission.

Revised and reprinted from *Letters From Maybe*, ISBN 0-7880-2349-7, printed in 2005 by CSS Publishing Company.

Library of Congress Cataloging-in-Publication Data

Pearson, Michael, 1948-
    Letters from maybe : true life letters from an imaginary town / Michael Pearson. — Rev. ed.
        p. cm.
    Includes indexes.
    ISBN-10: 0-7880-2613-5 (perfect bound : alk. paper)
    ISBN-13: 978-0-7880-2613-3 (perfect bound : alk. paper)
    1. Monologue sermons. 2. Imaginary letters. 3. United Methodist Church (U.S.)—Sermons. 4. Sermons, American—20th century. 5. Sermons, American—21st century. I. Title.
BV4307.M6P43 2009
251'.01—dc22

                                                            2008032129

For more information about CSS Publishing Company resources, visit our website at www.csspub.com or e-mail us at custserv@csspub.com or call (800) 241-4056.

ISBN-13: 978-0-7880-2613-3
ISBN-10: 0-7880-2613-5   PRINTED IN USA

*I dedicate this book
to my wife, Bethyl,
and my daughter, Kyla,
the real inspirations
in my life.*

Table Of Contents

Section 4: Two Years Ago

Section 5: Last Year

Preface

Lewis Carroll wrote about 97,000 letters in his lifetime, as well as a pamphlet called *Eight or Nine Wise Words about Letter-Writing*. He once said, "I'm beginning to think that the proper definition of 'Man' is 'an animal that writes letters.' "

Before you is a collection of letters that chronicle life in a small town. Written in what I hope you will find a humorous style, they present everyday situations in the imaginary setting of "Maybe." You'll find there America's first Refrigerator Magnet Museum, the original Pets 'n' Stuff, and many other places that exist only in fiction. Although the setting is imaginary, the events of graduation, county fairs, and weddings mirror real life.

The letters are presented as short parables, usually illustrating a point or two, and linked to one or two biblical passages. They have been used in a variety of settings over the past fifteen years. Originally read as meditations for communion services where there wasn't time for a full sermon, they have also been used in small groups, on planning retreats, and for training events. In worship, they are intended to present biblical truths and challenges in a fresh way to people who are familiar with the basic tenets of the Christian faith and the better-known Bible stories.

The place and characters are imaginary, and any resemblance to people living or deceased is purely coincidental, although many real people have been an encouragement to me. My parishioners in the Laingsburg and Middlebury United Methodist Churches and my colleagues in ministry at Tempe First United Methodist Church, Scottsdale United Methodist Church, Dove of the Desert United Methodist Church, and Velda Rose United Methodist Church have all been a source of inspiration and insight. *Esar's Comic Dictionary* (New York: Harvest House, 1943) has been a great help in supplying one-liners and puns used throughout the book. Above all, I thank the many people who have responded with laughter and occasional groans.

Michael Pearson
Mesa, Arizona

Section 1:
Five Years Ago

Salt And Light
January 2

Dear Mike,

Well, church got out late on Sunday. I didn't get too much out of the last half of the sermon. What is it Carl says? "Church starts at 11 o'clock sharp and finishes at 12:15 dull." I was wishing we could open a window. You know it's unhealthy to sleep in a stuffy room. But it was way too cold for opening any windows. Happily, the cold snap came just in time for Christmas.

I think most of us had pretty much completed our Christmas shopping well before Christmas. Some people get started earlier than others and some have the perfect gift that they can give year after year. Mike Wilson always gives his father a billfold. "The height of irony," Carl says. I do see the humor in it. Frankly, I don't like to wait 'til the last minute and can't really understand those who do. That's my complaint of long-standing.

Reverend Answers used to be one of the town's early shoppers. In fact, he liked to pretty well be done by the time he and Peggy decorated the parsonage for Christmas. There was a method to his madness. You see, he'd always hide their son, Bobby's, gifts in the boxes the decorations came out of and then simply haul the boxes back to the attic. There the gifts would await their grand entry under the tree on Christmas morning.

But last year Bobby discovered the hiding place. So perhaps it was understandable that Reverend Answers had put off shopping 'til the last minute. But it also put him off track for the rest of Christmas. As he drove back from Lansing about noon he tried to check off what else he needed to do for the Christmas Eve service, now just hours away.

As he pulled into the driveway of the parsonage he noticed the drizzle of rain had begun to freeze on the walk. It occurred to him that as mild as it had been up until that day there probably wasn't any salt for the walks at the church. A quick look in the basement proved he was right.

By the time he got to Lockwoods' hardware store they had already closed for Christmas Eve. So he went over to Bradley's Market. C. W. was just closing up.

"Sorry, we don't carry that kind of salt anymore," C. W. told Reverend Answers.

"Well, what do you carry?" Reverend Answers wanted to know.

"Only sea salt and kosher rock salt, nothing but the finest," C. W. enthused.

"How much is the rock salt?"

"Nine dollars for five pounds and the sea salt we only sell by the ounce, but listen, you don't want that salt. You've got a water softener; use the pellets."

"Aren't the pellets a little big?" Reverend Answers wondered aloud.

"Oh, just use a hammer to break them up."

"Does that work?"

"Sure, I use it all the time."

"Well, live and learn," Reverend Answers said as he was leaving the store. "And Merry Christmas," he quickly added.

That's how it was that Reverend Answers found himself in the church basement hammering away on salt pellets. He was feeling a bit frazzled, and perhaps more to the point, like there was something he still hadn't done. He was becoming anxious there wasn't time to do it, even if it suddenly came to him, which it did.

As he mounted the stairs and reached for the light switch he remembered what he'd forgotten. He raced home and got Peggy and Bobby to turn the house upside down searching for the Christmas Eve candlelight service candles. They turned up a few, but far from enough.

"I'm doing this as a Christmas favor," C. W. explained to Reverend Answers as he unlocked the door to the store. "And because it's Christmas, I'm not going to charge you for them. By the way, how did the salt work out?" he continued as they walked past the cash register.

"How many candles do you have?" Reverend Answers asked anxiously, fearing there wouldn't be enough.

"Well, all we have are these birthday candles," C. W. said as they reached the section of the store where the party supplies were kept.

"They'll have to do; give me every one," Reverend Answers said, panic rising in his voice.

"Even the ones that say 'Over-the-Hill'?" C. W. wanted to know. "You know it's better if you can make light of your problems," he added with a touch of whimsy in his voice.

Well, the candlelight service was certainly different this year. I got a candle in the shape of a five. Carl had a three and Coralie a zero. But I'll have to say they were a handy size, they didn't drip wax all over, they did lend a festive mood to the evening, and they kept Carl occupied suggesting what the numbers could represent. And it was tempting to put numbers together to evaluate the sermon, suggest the temperature outside, and even upcoming bowl scores. There was a warm glow to the whole church. In fact, I don't think the candlelight was ever gentler.

One of the Parker twins asked her mother, Charlene, "Just how old is Jesus anyway?" which was a fair question, I suppose. I'd guess somewhere in all those numbers we had the answer to that, too.

Carl kept saying next year he was going to special order the birthday candles that keep burning when you blow them out.

And thank you for the book you sent. I was pleased and surprised when I read the title in gilt on the spine *How-to-Hug* vol. 12. Of course I was disappointed when I realized it was only one slim volume of an encyclopedia. But I didn't let that stand in the way of giving out lots of hugs this Christmas.

Well, I'd better get this in the mail before Mr. Hurley, the mail carrier, gets here. We're praying for you.

Love to all,
Elizabeth

You are the salt of the earth. (Matthew 5:13a)
You are like a light for the world. (Matthew 5:14a)

13

Dear Mike,

Well, church got out late on Sunday. I didn't get too much out of the last half of the sermon. Someone asked Reverend Answers if there was too much "liberality" in the church these days, to which Reverend Answers replied, "Not in giving." Carl said Reverend Answers is a halting preacher, "He 'um-phasizes' every other word."

If the truth be known, I was distracted trying to imagine all that went on last weekend. Some folks around here had been complaining the church wasn't spiritual enough. To counteract that complaint or that trend, Reverend Answers decided to hold a men's retreat up at Houghton Lake. So last week Reverend Answers, Carl, and six other men from the church headed up to the church camp.

They left under bright skies Friday, both literally and in spirit. But before they got to Houghton Lake the skies had clouded over and the mood in Carl's car was a bit stormy, as it was discovered not one of the four was willing to sleep in the upper bunk. I think it was Billy who said it was his first trip that far north without a rifle. And I suppose that was about half true. But it did make all the other passengers wonder if maybe they shouldn't be sure to give Billy a lower bunk.

The camp director met them with the cheery news they'd have the whole place to themselves and that the cook would be in the following morning at six. The men could use the lodge/dining hall that evening — as long as they would be sure to turn off the lights. He and his wife were going to leave that evening to go into Traverse City. They'd be back midday Saturday, as they intended to shop for the camp and to see his mother-in-law.

I guess Reverend Answers began with a Bible study on spiritual gifts. But it didn't seem to be going very well, and he'd just about decided there was a "lack of spirituality" in at least seven people in the church, or at least a "giftedness." They turned in Friday night in not the best of spirits, only partially a reflection of the weather.

No one would say it was revenge, but the three men in Reverend Answers' cabin, Carl, John, and Walt, found out that he was a sound sleeper. As Carl noted, "Sleep and the world sleeps with you, but snore and you sleep alone." Evidently, Reverend Answers can really snore. Carl told them to think of it as sheet music, and also noted that snoring was an unfavorable report from headquarters.

Finally, everyone must have "drifted off" again. Because when Reverend Answers awoke at 6:00, after what could only be described as a restful, pleasant night's sleep — a pleasure that he alone enjoyed (the same could be said for his snoring, I suppose), he was surprised by the snow that had fallen during the night, at least two feet. Moreover, it had drifted up against the cabin, and the snow was still falling and still drifting. Most surprising of all, Walt was missing from his bunk.

After rousing Carl and John to see if they knew where Walt was, a certain panic began to form in the mind of each. Had Walt gone out to the toilets? Was he up in the kitchen dining hall? In the next cabin with the others? Finally, John asked the unthinkable. "What if he wandered off in the snowstorm, got lost, sat down in a snowbank, and fell asleep?" It was cold, very cold that night. "He does have a heart condition, you know," he volunteered. They spent the better part of two hours searching high and low before realizing not only was Walt missing but the storm had closed the road into camp, and for that matter, out. Nor was the cook coming unless he had sled dogs.

Fortunately, the problem of Walt's disappearance solved itself when he appeared coming out of the camp office where he'd retreated around midnight to find a quiet place to sleep, on the couch in the office.

The cook did call to say it was impossible to get out to the camp, as even the highway was closed — but it would probably open tomorrow or Monday. Carl volunteered to try his hand at cooking. Actually, it proved to be something of a challenge as there wasn't much on hand: some flour, sugar, shortening, a few cans of peaches, oatmeal, evaporated milk, and so forth.

15

Actually, Carl did pretty well, but by Monday evening everyone was getting tired of hearing Carl call them to dinner with the words, "Donner party of eight," "Donner party of seven," "Donner party of six."

Although the camp manager called several times, he, too, was unable to get back until the snowplow opened the two-mile dirt road into camp. He suggested the men get the camp tractor running and begin plowing the camp road down to the county road.

The men were pretty sure the only thing wrong with the tractor was the battery, which had run down through inactivity. But they had no way to jump it, as it was six-volt and the cars were twelve, so they decided to see if they could push start it. The problem was trying to push in the snow. It was impossible to get enough traction to get up to a speed to turn over the engine.

You'll recall how the camp is laid out. The lodge is on a small rise overlooking Houghton Lake, with the cabins lining the lakeshore below. I guess it was Billy who suggested if they push the tractor up to the lodge, they could roll it down hill and pop the clutch as it gathered sufficient speed.

Their success was short-lived. The old John Deere coughed to life halfway down the hill. Unfortunately, Carl was unable to stop it before the front two tires broke through the ice at water's edge. Trying to back it out only served to dig the rear tires in about half way to the hubs, a humbling experience to say the least.

This did have a positive benefit that was apparent to Reverend Answers during the Bible studies. Perhaps trying to offset any displeasure the camp manager might have at finding his tractor halfway into the lake, Carl got all the men to repaint the kitchen and give it a thorough cleaning. This was a perfect time, he reasoned, "No food was being prepared in it." No one would have argued with him, although the cook did come out Monday by snowmobile with a few items and that tided them over 'til Wednesday when they were finally plowed out.

According to Carl, the highlight was Sunday night's meal: oatmeal and ice cream. I guess Carl had found a few tins of sweetened condensed milk (something he swears comes from Arizona), so they concocted a peach "snow ice cream." By all accounts it did put everyone in a pretty good mood after a rather testy day, a day in which all of them expected to be on the way home to their own beds. Speaking of beds, by Saturday night Reverend Answers was in a private cabin where he could snore as loud as he liked.

Maybe most important they all did have a lot of quiet time, both night and day. The snow muffled all the sounds outside, and the time with the Bible and away from the routine of home muffled most of the inner ones. However, there is nothing like a tractor in a lake to quiet an ego. You'd be surprised what they heard when they listened.

Well, I'd better get this in the mail before Mr. Hurley, the mail carrier, gets here. We're praying for you and that congregation.

> Love to all,
> Elizabeth

Retreat/Humility

For thus says the high and lofty one who inhabits eternity, whose name is Holy: I dwell in the high and holy place, and also with those who are contrite and humble in spirit. (Isaiah 57:15a)

Be still, and know that I am God! I am exalted among the nations, I am exalted in the earth. (Psalm 46:10)

Dear Mike,

Well, church got out late on Sunday. I didn't get too much out of the last half of the sermon. Reverend Answers has just returned from a continuing education event on preaching and he's started in on gesturing vigorously and walking around during the sermon. Carl says they taught all the preachers that a moving target is harder to hit. Really Reverend Answers usually has a good train of thought. It just takes it too long to get to the terminal.

If the truth be known, I think all of us were having trouble paying attention to Reverend Answers, what with being distracted with two first-time visitors. Several things suggested that this was not only their first time to our church, but also their first time to any church. They arrived a couple minutes past eleven, he holding on to her hand more for moral support, I suppose, than to help him along. They walked right up to the front pew. (Now if that isn't a tip-off to never being at church before, I don't know what is.)

The sanctuary was filled with sunlight Sunday and the old oak pews glowed like honey. The whole sanctuary was giving off a warm, friendly glow. At least that's what I hope the two felt as they sat there, Lacey Hodges, age ten or eleven and her half-brother, Ryan Cormaki, age seven.

Of course, all of us know them, or, more correctly, know something about them. We see them around town. We know some of their story, although I'm afraid we know mostly the harder parts of that story, or, more correctly, the harder parts of their mother's story.

It was cute to see them sitting there, nervously leaning in to each other. In fact, looking at her hands gave another mute testimony to the fact that this was their first time inside a church. Lacey was wearing gloves, white gloves, white dress gloves, gloves that were just a little too big for her hands, gloves that I recognized as having at one time graced my own hands.

Carl said after the service that nowadays if you see a woman in church with gloves, you wonder if she's trying not to leave fingerprints. I'd half expected him to say to Lacey after church, "You can take your gloves off; you'll feel better without them." Fortunately, he didn't. One can only wonder what old movie, book, or television show Lacey had seen to put it in her mind that white gloves and church went together.

I had last seen the gloves in October. I had cleaned out some things for the Fall Harvest Bazaar and had donated them as rummage.

I think I wrote how, for the first time in anyone's memory, we lost money on the bazaar. I believe we could have recovered from the setback of having a locksmith drive out from Lansing and open the church office where several women's purses were locked up for safekeeping, and the keys had gone to Detroit or someplace in Reverend Answers' pocket. But the hit we took when Myra June, the organist, realized her shoes, the $280 soft kidskin shoes, shoes she's waited *years* to own — her emphasis, not mine — shoes that are made specifically for playing the organ, had been inadvertently picked up from the floor near the organ and placed on the clothing rummage table and sold for a penny on the dollar. You can see how our profits were doomed. The shoes were now costing well over $300.

In all the commotion, I don't guess any of us really knew who'd purchased what. So I was thrilled to see those gloves back at church. They'd only been there once before and that was more years ago than I care to remember.

Do you know how I was so sure they were mine? I'd had to darn a couple of moth holes in them before I put them in the rummage sale. As Carl would say, "How does a moth live? — it eats nothing but holes." I hadn't darned anything in years. On the topic of darning, Carl likes to point out how times have changed by noting, "It used to be a woman darned her husband's socks. Now she socks her darned husband." But all in all I suppose that's progress.

And it used to be that children weren't bold enough to venture out to unfamiliar places on their own, even church. At least I wasn't.

I wore those gloves as a fifteen-year-old at my father's funeral. And I'd kept them all this time, moving them from drawer to drawer, occasionally coming across them and letting them take

19

me back over the years. They were a magic carpet for my memories, carrying me along, often to this very church and the few times I'd sat in the front pew, always funerals. We mark time in funny ways. You know what I mean. We mark it by people's deaths. You might say the times we were in the front row. We'll reflect, "Now let's see, wasn't that the year Walter died?" or "Was that the spring that Esther died?" Too seldom do we reckon time when things begin.

"I was admiring your gloves," I said to Lacey.

"Oh, thank you," she replied, as polite as could be.

"I forgot mine at home today. It was careless of me," I continued. "I hope you'll wear yours again next Sunday. I'm sure I'll remember mine."

Mike, you can't believe how hard it is to find dress gloves anymore. I spent Tuesday calling around. Interestingly, several places mentioned I was the third or fourth call they'd had in the last two days. By Thursday I'd resigned myself to wearing a pair of tan goatskin driving gloves if I couldn't find something better before Sunday.

Anyway, I'm going to refer to this year as the year a girl came to church for the first time, sat in the front row, and got us wearing gloves again. And a much older girl saw her times in the front row in a new light, not just a time of ending but of beginning.

Now, I don't suppose gloves would catch on out where you live. Well, I'd better get this in the mail before Mr. Hurley, the mail carrier, gets here. We're praying for you and your congregation.

Love to all,
Elizabeth

Welcoming visitors/Memorial
Welcome one another, therefore, just as Christ has welcomed you, for the glory of God. (Romans 15:7)

... then you shall tell them that the waters of the Jordan were cut off in front of the ark of the covenant of the Lord. When it crossed over the Jordan, the waters of the Jordan were cut off. So these stones shall be to the Israelites a memorial forever. (Joshua 4:7)

Pigeons At Easter
April 7

Dear Mike,

Well, church got out late on Sunday. I didn't get too much out of the last half of the sermon. It seems a pastor's words are never done. I think the sermon was what Carl calls a "worn-out shoe sermon — the sole was gone but the tongue kept wagging."

Well, if the truth be known I was distracted from above. I guess that needs some explaining, now, doesn't it?

This all began when Reverend Answers went out to Garden Grove, California, to Robert Schuller's workshop, "Possibility Thinking in the Third Millennium." Reverend Answers came back with a new vision. I shouldn't complain, as most of the ideas seem pretty good. The sign out front, which used to say, "All Denominations Welcome" (and which Carl was forever amending with "... but $20s preferred"), now reads "Welcome Home." And it does look like we're expecting company what with the way the daffodils, forsythia, and hyacinth are in bloom. Lonnie has even put a fresh coat of paint on the front door.

On the other hand, we've all heard Reverend Answers say, "We don't have a problem here, we have an opportunity," about as much as we can stand. A little of this possibility stuff goes a long way.

But the most radical idea he picked up was this emphasis on using the dramatic, the theatrical, and the visual to get his message across. I guess the thinking is if you're going to have a vision you have to be able to see it. So Reverend Answers has been trying to put more of that into his sermons. At least, that was, until Easter.

One thing that Reverend Answers picked up out in Garden Grove was the idea of releasing doves on Easter. That was something at least Reverend Answers could visualize: doves rising gracefully in flight at the conclusion of the services, circling the church once, maybe twice, and winging heavenward. Now that would be dramatic, or so he thought.

At the end of the Easter service Reverend Answers invited the children to join him down in front. In previous years, this was the place in the service where he gave each child an Easter egg. But rather than eggs this year he produced a big, dark gray cardboard box labeled "Tomb." At first I misread it "Bomb" (which as it turned out wasn't too far off).

Reverend Answers had everyone's attention as he marched the length of the aisle, carrying the box in front of him, and trailing children behind like he was a modern-day pied piper. He stopped just outside the door and gathered the children around on the porch. He set the box down, opened it, and about a dozen pigeons lifted off in unison. The effect on the children was instantaneous and to be expected. They grabbed for the birds screaming with unleashed glee. The effect on the birds was also instantaneous and to be expected; although these were homing pigeons, they had never been subjected to this type of welcome or departure. They scattered. Whether by chance or guided by some unseen hand, two darted back into the church, only to be greeted by more screams, just an octave lower in pitch and perhaps a tad less enthusiastic. Of course this only drove the poor, panic-stricken pigeons to flap about with greater effort.

By now the children were back in the sanctuary imagining that this was still part of the children's sermon and that they might still get an Easter egg. Most of the adults were praying if eggs came, or anything else for that matter, that it wouldn't be delivered by the birds. The pair finally found a roost on the cornice over the stained-glass windows of Peter and Paul. If you looked at them just right it seemed as if they were sculpted into the woodwork.

Calm was finally restored and church let out. Reverend Answers called the owner of the pigeons, Abe Sorda, who lives over in Chapin, and was told to open the front door and turn off all the lights in the building and eventually they'd fly to the light and leave.

Tuesday he called Reverend Answers to say the birds hadn't found their way home and to inquire if they were still locked up in the church. I guess it was Thursday when Lonnie figured out the birds were still at the church, cooped up in the belfry. The belfry had been screened over when the bell was taken out a few years ago to prevent pigeons from getting in and nesting up there. Of course no one had imagined a pair might enter from the sanctuary. So our pair had been trapped up there for four days when Lonnie finally got up on the roof and opened up the screen. One bird shot out of there like a cat was after it but the other was sitting on an old nest. When Lonnie lifted her aside there were two little eggs.

Reverend Answers is now the proud owner of what the man from over at Chapin refers to as a "nesting pair." He thinks he might be able to retrieve them after the squealers are flying. But for the meantime they're ours. Pigeons mate for life and "home" to either mate or chicks, and in this case the couple was together, found a nest, and just stayed put. The male does make a racket when we're in the building. We sure know they're upstairs.

Last Sunday Carl asked Reverend Answers if he thought Robert Schuller ever had an opportunity like this.

All in all it was kind of nice. I mean we've got pigeons in the belfry, two additional Easter eggs, and more excitement than we've had here in years. As Carl says, "It's not every Easter you get yells, bells, and smells, or 'oohing and cooing.' "

I'd better get this in the mail before Mr. Hurley, the mail carrier, gets here. We're praying for you.

Love to all,
Elizabeth

We humans make plans, but the Lord has final word. (Proverbs 16:1 CEV)

Dear Mike,

Well, church got out late on Sunday. I didn't get too much out of the last half of the sermon. Reverend Answers has the gift of taking the eternal gospel and making an everlasting sermon. Carl says the difference between a good sermon and a bad sermon is a comfortable nap. And if the truth be known, I dozed off somewhere near the middle.

It's been awfully dry here, and I don't mean just in church.

The dryness has really aggravated the dust on the dirt and gravel roads out here in the country. Ordinarily I wouldn't complain, but the road commission has about a mile and a half of Doyle Road torn up, which necessitates me, and most of us who live out this way, using "an alternative route," which means about four miles of dirt and dust.

And I'm not the only one upset by the inconvenience. There's been lots of grousing down at the Busy-Bee Café about the road commission's repair work this spring. There are detours all over the county, but it seems like around here it's always the worst. Carl says the detour is the roughest line between two points.

Mike, it's hard not to think we've been singled out, when you consider this town poses a special challenge to the highway people. I'll admit we do make extra work for them, albeit unintentionally. You know the signs: Lansing 28, Maybe 13, or East Lansing 18, Maybe 6. I've heard people theorize down at the Busy-Bee that college students use the signs as dorm decorations. But I'd bet you could find half a dozen in barns and garages on Doyle Road between here and town.

"Maybe" has always been something of a curse and a blessing for us here since the town was named. At least twice a year we awake to find the Baptist church sign abridged to read; "Maybe Baptist, Maybe Not." Usually this happens after a sermon on some doctrinal point, my assumption being the sign is altered by a disgruntled member, who lives three farms over from me.

Several years before you were here, we changed the name of the United Methodist church from Maybe First United Methodist for the same reason. And realistically, what are the chances of there being a Maybe Second? Anyway, Maybe Hope has just the right ring to my ear.

But back to the road commission, we do want our town mentioned on the highway signs. We're a town that can live with ambiguity better than anonymity, I guess. So they are forever being called out to replace the purloined signs.

Blaine, the owner of the Refrigerator Magnet Museum, was in the Busy-Bee last Tuesday morning seeking advice. He and Carolyn were having their eighteenth anniversary Friday, and he was looking for gift suggestions. He needed a really good gift as he's been an absentee husband/father the past month and will be until Labor Day.

During the late spring, the Refrigerator Magnet Museum is very busy getting ready for the summer season. The detours will slow people down, and might even dissuade some from visiting. But on Tuesday, Blaine had another problem on his mind.

"Any suggestions for an anniversary gift?" Blaine asked no one in particular.

"I've always found just remembering our anniversary is a big surprise to Coralie," Carl offered. "How about a housedress? They're seldom worn out," he continued, warming to the subject. "Miss it and you'll catch it later," Carl shouted as Blaine walked out the door.

But Tuesday evening, Blaine found himself at one of the shops on the edge of campus that caters to coeds. He finally settled on a jacket, blouse, and slacks outfit: very colorful, very youthful, very expensive. He even liked the name of the company that made them. "Cut Loose." "Now that's the spirit!" Blaine thought to himself.

"Cut Loose" didn't convey that same breakout imagery for Carolyn. When she unwrapped the box Saturday morning at breakfast and read the label she started sobbing.

This was sure not the effect Blaine was hoping for. Perhaps Carl's right. A housedress might be a better idea, he thought to himself.

"I know I've put on a few pounds lately but ..." Carolyn trailed off into tears.

"Try it on. You'll look great in it," Blaine began.

"Well, okay," Carolyn said in a resigned voice. At least he cared. And she had heard, "You'll look great...." And, in fact, she did.

"See 'Cut Loose' is a mind set, not a sewing term," Blaine tried to explain, finally catching on.

She decided to wear it Saturday night when they went out to dinner at the Heritage House up in Ovid where they've gone the last sixteen years. When the hostess asked if this was a "special occasion," she knew it looked good on her.

"Want to go any place special?" Blaine asked after dinner.

"Maybe!" Carolyn replied.

Well, I'd better get this in the mail before Mr. Hurley, the mail carrier, gets here. We're praying for you and your church.

Love to all,
Elizabeth

I want their hearts to be encouraged and united in love, so that they may have all the riches of assured understanding and have the knowledge of God's mystery, that is, Christ himself. (Colossians 2:2)

Refrigerator Magnet Museum
June 3

Dear Mike,

Well, church got out late on Sunday. I didn't get too much out of the last half of the sermon. Carl said, "All work and no plagiarism makes for a dull sermon." But I suppose I was distracted by the weather.

The weather has been real nice lately. What I'd call good sleeping weather — warm days and cool nights. I guess everybody's pretty much got his or her garden in by now. I'm planting more flowers and fewer vegetables now that I'm not canning as much. I don't think anyone is putting up as much as they used to.

But we still talk a good game. It was the number one topic of conversation at Thelma's Cut 'n' Curl. You remember their motto: "Where the men are rare and the women are well done." Although I've cut back some, I think most people have gone pretty much overboard on planting again this year. Don't get me wrong, I'm sympathetic. You never know, sometimes so little actually produces good fruit. And each year there is more anxiety as more and more of us have privately decided not to use pesticides. Of course, we're afraid to go public with our plan in case we have a bad Japanese beetle infestation again and we fall off the wagon.

We're all trying to hedge our bets by composting. And I collected several praying mantis egg cases from the pond down by the Doyles' farm. Seems like we're all trying to simplify our lives but it's pretty complex. It's like we're all starting over.

Speaking of something simple, did you realize this is the tenth anniversary of the Refrigerator Magnet Museum? You may recall Blaine Richardson. I guess you'd say Blaine was Maybe's original "hippie." He'd probably tried fifteen or twenty different jobs since he graduated from high school thirty-some years ago.

I sure think part of his being a dreamer was being Blair's younger brother. I'm sure you'll remember Blair. It must be hard to live in someone like Blair's shadow. Blair was valedictorian — I guess Blaine was lucky to graduate. Blair was good at sports and music. Blaine, well, I heard was about fourth chair trumpet (out of

27

four in the marching band) and didn't participate in sports as far as I can recall. And as if that weren't enough, Blair could fix about anything. Blaine could break about anything.

Blair's about the best vet we ever had around here. Along with everything else, he's good with animals. Blaine's been in and out of town over the years, usually when he's between jobs. Which as I said, I doubt if anyone could give a very precise accounting of.

I do recall he even had a tanning salon a few years back. Carl used to say, "Who'd go pay for a suntan when it was yours for the basking?" Well, that was about it. The men around here tan from the neck up and the elbow down. One of the bachelors who farms out in Seels Township asked no one in particular at the Busy-Bee Café, "Why would you want a tan where nobody was going to see it?" The point being around here an overall tan would be taken as a sign of unemployment, if not downright laziness.

More than that, the tanning equipment kept breaking down. Blaine would call Blair to come see if he could fix it. Finally, in exasperation, Blair told Blaine, "Find a job where the equipment can't break!"

Well, that set Blaine to thinking about what, if anything, wouldn't break down. What couldn't break down? It finally dawned on him — magnets. Well, once he had that idea things kind of snowballed for him. First, he started marketing refrigerator magnets in the shape of the most popular refrigerators; sort of a Ray Bradbury *Illustrated Man* type of thing. Then he branched out into refrigerator magnets shaped like magnets. You know the horseshoe ones, red with black tips. He did real well selling magnets at craft shows, and wholesaling to florists and gift shops — so well, that he hired a few friends to help make and sell them.

Well, ten years ago this month, Blaine opened America's First Refrigerator Magnet Museum. It is laid out really nice with doors of refrigerators lining the walls and on each door hundreds of magnets. It's all divided up. There's a historical section with what he believes were the forerunners of today's refrigerator magnet. Do you remember those black and white Scottie dogs? Blaine thinks they were among the original ones.

Of course, there's a fruit and vegetable section, homemade section, *trompe l'oeil* (that trick your eye), flowers and bows, messages, sports teams, cartoon figures, advertising, homemade, and messages from the Bible — it just goes on and on as far as the eye can see. And did you know that America is the only country with refrigerator magnets? It's true; he wanted a foreign section but wasn't able to find any.

And after the articles in the Lansing and Detroit papers and the feature on "Entertainment Tonight," it was just nonstop traffic. They've expanded the building once and the parking lot twice. Of course, Blaine sells magnets right out of the museum showroom and the snack bar is a real moneymaker, too.

We're all real happy for him. And he's the same old Blaine. Just the other day in the Busy-Bee Café I heard him say when someone asked him how he was doing that he still had problems, but he was just happy they weren't the same ones as ten years ago.

Well, I'd better get this in the mail before Mr. Hurley, the mail carrier, gets here. We're all praying for you and your church.

Love to all,
Elizabeth

Fruit of the Spirit
By contrast, the fruit of the Spirit is love, joy, peace, patience, kindness, generosity, faithfulness. (Galatians 5:22)

Dear Mike,

Well, church got out late on Sunday. I didn't get too much out of the last half of the sermon. For the first time in my life I actually envied my feet. They were asleep. Carl says, "Reverend Answers has been preaching like an angel. He's harping on us."

Our weather has been good, but it doesn't seem to cool off at night the way it used to. I'm looking forward to a great fall and here it is only July. Lately Carl has been saying, "The bigger the vacation, the harder the fall."

If it's true, I can only imagine what kind of fall Dwight and Arlene are in for. Did I mention how this past month was their 35th wedding anniversary? To celebrate, they decided to take one of those Princess Cruises to the Caribbean. You know they've had a good marriage to withstand the hardships of being partners at the Busy-Bee Café all these years. Together they've been able to multiply the joys and divide the troubles. Carl says at the café the relationship is "Dwight is the treasurer and Arlene is the treasury." What can I say? You know how good her cooking is.

Darlene, the waitress, and the new cook, Rex, threw a little bon voyage party for them a couple weeks ago. Rex made a big sheet cake with a picture of the *Titanic* drawn on it. All day people stopped in to wish them well and have some cake and coffee.

Carl held forth most of the afternoon with jokes and quips. Someone might comment on how cruises were for the wealthy and Carl would agree, "Yes, many who are sick on board are well off."

Or someone might say how beautiful the days at sea are, to which Carl would say, "Yes, that's true, the days are either gorgeous or disgorgeous."

Another mentioned seasickness and Carl said, "I hope Dwight and Arlene will be able to contain themselves. After all, this isn't the outward bound program they've signed up for."

And so it went most of the afternoon. You can imagine how relieved Dwight and Arlene were to fly to Nassau.

The five-day cruise began under a cloud (as if the send off from town wasn't enough of one). It was a cloud named Bill to be exact. Hurricane Bill was hundreds of miles away but the skies upon boarding were overcast. Dwight said they were kind of a brindled color. Not exactly an auspicious beginning.

By dinner that first night, some of Carl's comments seemed positively prophetic. People were playing hide and sick. The sea was rough — which actually was a relief to Dwight.

You see, Arlene had her heart set on dancing after dinner each night. Dwight thought that with all the pitching and listing if he stepped on Arlene's toes, he could blame the ocean. In fact, that night the term rock music took on a whole new meaning for the passengers. Most everyone retired early. Someone said, during one number, the band was playing Gershwin and Gershwin was losing.

By noon, it was obvious that not only was the band affected by the rolling seas but at least one other key crew member was, too. The Princess line had hired a new chef from Miami and this was to be his introduction to shipboard cooking. Unfortunately, he had a career-ending ailment — motion sickness.

The purser and one of the galley assistants gamely took over. Most people had lost their appetites by then anyway. By dinner on day two it was obvious that thoughts of mutiny had entered the minds of not a few passengers.

As one fellow so succinctly put it, "Our problem is we've got a chef who can cook but won't and a purser who can't cook and will." Of course, Arlene and Dwight didn't feel that way. In fact, Arlene always says food tastes better when someone else cooks it. They were among the handful of people who were really enjoying the cruise. Dwight was almost beginning to enjoy the dancing.

On the third day, Arlene presented herself to the purser and volunteered to help with the cooking. Weak tea, dry toast, and poached eggs were the first order of business. By lunch, she was pretty well acquainted with the kitchen, and the chicken dumpling soup, melon compote, and refrigerator rolls with marmalade were a big hit.

That all took place on Wednesday. And I bet you can still remember that Wednesday night at the Busy-Bee features meatloaf, mashed potatoes, and garden fresh peas as the Blue Plate Special. Well, it's hard to break lifelong habits. She was delighted the filet mignon ground up to such a nice meatloaf. Although she did think it would have been better if they'd had a few onion soup mixes on board.

The last two days the weather was some better. The chef felt well enough to return to the kitchen. Dwight and Arlene ate at the captain's table the rest of the cruise. And happily the thankful captain and crew kept Arlene busy on the dance floor.

I suppose you could say it was a "busman's holiday," but they really looked great when they returned last week.

"If a cruise doesn't make you forget your troubles at least seasickness does," Dwight said.

Last Friday, a letter arrived from the Princess Cruise Lines thanking Arlene and offering her a job as chef. They've framed it and put it up on the wall by the first dollar they made.

What is it that Carl says? "Ocean travel brings out what's inside." So it does.

I'd better get this in the mail before Mr. Hurley, the mail carrier, gets here. We're praying for you and your congregation.

Love to all,
Elizabeth

Discipleship
*As he walked by the Sea of Galilee, he saw two brothers, Simon, who is called Peter, and Andrew his brother, casting a net into the sea — for they were fishermen. And he said to them, "Follow me, and I will make you fish for people." * (Matthew 4:18-19)

Dear Mike,

Well, church got out late on Sunday. I didn't get too much out of the last half of the sermon. Carl always says a good definition of a sermon is *angel food*. If the truth be told, my mind was on cakes instead of the sermon. Cakes and the county fair and the fact I'd been shut out of a blue ribbon in not one but two of my best categories.

I always look forward to the fair. It got underway with the parade. The high school band played well, as usual, in spite of the wool uniforms and the heat. I'd been busy getting my entries ready for the homemaking arts category the entire week prior to the fair. The entries had to be at the demonstration building Sunday evening.

This year I'd limited myself to just two entries. One was bread and butter pickles, and the other was a new turtle cake. I use a sour cream cake base with a pecan, caramel, and chocolate topping.

Now I'm not one to brag, but both have had very favorable reviews at our church potlucks. I figure I'm doing well to get compliments from some of the men. After all, men have been complaining about the food served to them since Adam.

The pickles were judged Sunday night. There is a woman from over at Chapin who has won the pickle competition at least ten times over the years. The best I've ever done is second place. But this year I felt I had put up the winning pickles. You know pickles are judged like diamonds — on the four Cs: crispness, color, clarity of the brine, and components of taste (not too sweet, not too sour). Coralie always says pickles reflect the maker's personality more than any other food. And I can't argue the point; after all, I never was good at dills. I had discovered this new alum last year, and I felt sure it would give me the crispness I needed to go over the top at this year's fair.

Monday I took in the cake for Tuesday's judging. I went over about noon. I felt so confident that I lingered around the midway before going into the demonstration building. I even had a corn dog to celebrate!

Can you imagine my disappointment? That Chapin woman won the blue ribbon again. Not only that, I didn't even get runner-up. My pickles were wrapped up in white — third place! I just dropped off my cake and headed home. I knew I had a pretty good chance for a blue ribbon in the cake category. But a cake doesn't really reflect much of the baker's personality, even with sour cream. I was sure I'd be in a better mood Tuesday. Carl says, "Failure is the path of least persistence." But I was just about to give up on bread and butter pickles and take up dills.

Tuesday I got to the fairgrounds early. I was already enjoying the enraptured looks my cake was sure to bring to the judges' faces. In the demonstration building I couldn't locate my cake anyplace. I began to fear that it had met with some foul play, dropped by a careless helper, or worse, stolen by a jealous competitor.

It had met with foul play all right. On Monday night there was a power outage, and in the darkness, two boar hogs had gotten loose from the 4-H barn. One evidently had sniffed and snorted his way into the demonstration building. As I imagine it, he made a beeline for my cake. He had finished one cake when his escape was detected, and he was apprehended. One cake! I went home with a headache.

Coralie said someday I'd see the humor in this. I hope so. In the meantime, I told Coralie a sense of humor is what makes you laugh at something that would make you mad if it happened to you.

Carl and Coralie have been telling everyone it was obvious I had the best cake. After all, which one did the hog go after in the midst of all those cakes? Well, there were no posthumous awards in the cake category.

By Friday I was feeling some better about the whole mess. I even felt good enough to go to the 4-H stock auction that after-noon. I'll admit I was happy that Bradley's Market in town had the winning bid on Jo-Jo, the rogue hog that had eaten my cake. I got Lee Bradley aside and ordered ten pounds of sausage. I'm go-ing to enjoy some real good breakfasts this fall.

Carl called and said, "A hog has to be killed before it can be cured." Where does he get those? At any rate, that's one hog cured of eating cake.

Lee Bradley said he'd have the sausage ready this week.

I'd better get this in the mail before Mr. Hurley, the mail carrier, gets here. We're praying for you and your congregation.

Love to all,
Elizabeth

Pride
Pride goes before destruction, and a haughty spirit before a fall.
(Proverbs 16:18)

Festival Of The Water Tower
September 4

Dear Mike,

Well, church got out late on Sunday. I didn't get too much out of the last half of the sermon. Carl says Reverend Answers needs no introduction, but a conclusion would be a blessing. You know, once again, I envied my feet — they were asleep.

If the truth be known, my mind wasn't on the sermon, but rather on the rest of our four-day weekend. I think you'll remember how the town celebrates Labor Day on the first Monday in September, and then the following day we celebrate the Festival of the Water Tower. This year is our 46th celebration, although it hardly seems like it was that long ago that it got started.

I can still remember the fights people had before the water tower was erected. You know how the town, for the most part, sits in the Chemung Valley with the lake just northwest of town. The lake, being fed by several springs, including one artesian, has provided water for the townspeople for generations. I can recall as a child there would be days when the spearmint that grew along the water's edge near the springs during the summer would actually flavor the water.

After World War II, people started putting up homes out south of town on the hills. Out there they had to put in wells for water as the town's water system and pump wouldn't deliver water that distance.

I don't think the well water out there was ever very tasty, certainly no "hint-of-mint" — more like a whiff of sulfur. But in 1952, the folks out on Doyle and Cutter Roads went from bad water to no water as wells went dry literally overnight. Geologists said a limestone plate collapsed in the Albion Aquifer and completely diverted the water at eighty feet, so wells would need to be drilled at 400-plus depth. As Carl would later say, "The wells were tried (dried) and found wanting."

Well, the people south of town started talking up a water tower. Needless to say, the idea was met with less than enthusiasm by the town dwellers, who already had a water works that delivered the aforementioned mint water.

Twice, a plebiscite rejected the idea of expanding the town's water system to include the forty or so homes, at that time, on the hill. "It is just too costly," went the argument. Or "If they want town water, let them move to town." Or "We already paid for this system; if they want one, let them pay for it. We've done our part."

It looked like a real impasse until one of the Bradley men said he'd heard about a town down near Detroit that had a water tower they were getting rid of as the town had outgrown it. The price was right: haul it away.

One thing led to another and before too long the town had a water tower up on the rise over town. But no one would go the cost of the pump and the existing one was just too small. "Let the people south of town pay for the pump if they want water," or so went the argument. Of course, those were the people least able to afford it. And that was the way things were until one of the Alto women heard that the pumps at the Soo Locks in the Upper Peninsula were being replaced and municipalities could requisition one.

So during the summer of 1952, the town pulled together to install the pump and build a pump house, dig the trenches, lay the pipes, and hook up the pipes to the tower and to the homes.

Labor Day being a holiday was set as the day the water would be turned on. It was clear, warm, with gentle breezes blowing, a perfect day, although the turnout for the turn-on was modest, inasmuch as most people wanted to be home to witness the miracle rather than see the mayor throw a switch.

The few who were there claim the water tower actually swelled like a balloon when the pump was turned on. At any rate the pump, designed to pump tens of thousands of gallons per minute, just about overinflated the water tower. And although it creaked, groaned, and, if some witnesses are to be believed, swelled to half again its size, it held. Of course, it put the water under tremendous pressure.

People cheered, others yelled. Those yelling represented the group who were home watching pipes burst, toilet tanks fill to overflowing, and kitchen faucets flying skyward to propulsion rates seldom achieved outside of rocket launches, two or three of whom still claim to have plumbing objects imbedded in walls and ceilings.

This, of course, was much more pronounced in the older homes in town, homes whose plumbing had only previously carried water at something just over two pounds per square inch.

It must have been thirty minutes before people realized exactly what was happening. One great advantage of the old Soo pump was it pumped in reverse just as fast. The tower was emptied.

Of course, now no one had water, which, unfortunately, was in great demand for clean-up in the sixty or so homes in town whose pipes and fittings had exploded. The water was delivered at about sixty pounds per square inch, exactly the same pressure found in most champagne bottles. Unfortunately, most of the old homes were equipped for softer drinks.

Up on the hill, with the new plumbing, people were wildly enthusiastic until the water stopped completely, and they learned the reason for its sudden disappearance.

It was those people who started the tradition of the Festival of the Water Tower. They worked all that day and the next, most taking off work, cleaning the houses of those in town, mopping up kitchens and baths, replumbing whole houses, finding leaks, bringing in food and water; they were in the habit — they'd been hauling it for weeks and months.

These days, of course, the day after Labor Day is spent with lots of festivities. I'm still fond of the water balloon toss and the bathtub race up the hill to the tower always draws a crowd. The best thing of all is that we all turn out to help those less fortunate, sometimes those in town, sometimes those on the hill. Those who, unfortunately, remain among those least able to afford it, but we all help each other.

No need to rush this to the mailbox. Mr. Hurley, the mail carrier, won't be making deliveries or pickups today as he celebrates the Festival of the Water Tower like the whole town by calling in and saying he's got water on the knee, or brain, I can't remember which.

We're praying for you and your church.

Love to all,
Elizabeth

Community/Discipleship
And the king will answer them, "Truly I tell you, just as you did it to one of the least of these who are members of my family, you did it to me." (Matthew 25:40)

Dear Mike,

Well, church got out late on Sunday. I didn't get too much out of the last half of the sermon. Some of our members have taken to comparing Reverend Answers to Jonathan Edwards; when he finishes a sermon there is always a great awakening.

We do have the new sign up out in front of the church, but there has been more than a little discussion as to what to put on it. You see, there is a place on the sign where you can use removable letters and write your special message, sermon title, or announce an upcoming event. Several ideas have been put forward. The United Methodist Women, who bought and paid for the sign, think it ought to advertise the upcoming Harvest Bazaar. Orlan saw a church sign over in Lansing that said, "Ch--ch, what's missing? UR" and he's been trying to get the trustees behind him.

"After all," he says, "we installed it!"

Carl, representing no particular interest group, has suggested "Free Faith Lifts."

Of course Reverend Answers has been pushing pretty hard for the title of the upcoming sermon. But, Mike, I ask you, is it appropriate to put up something like last Sunday's sermon title, "The Holy Spirit Isn't a Medium. It's a Large?" (I don't even know if that would be appropriate at Pentecost.) Needless to say, our council board meetings have been pretty lively of late, but nothing to compare with the board meetings the Fairchilds have had to endure lately.

I'm sure I wrote to you on how successful their store had become, and famous, too. They were bought out by that syndicate from Detroit and the syndicate has been franchising stores throughout the Midwest. Of course, Henry and Helen have held on to the store here in town. It is amazing that they've done so well. But it hasn't gone to their heads.

Well, really all they did was combine their two hobbies. But like peanut butter and chocolate, the chemistry was right. You know Helen has always had a way with animals. I've never seen one that just didn't immediately take to her. And I guess, in his own way Henry has a flair for taxidermy. But a combination pet store and taxidermy shop? Who would have thought it would have caught on?

Carl used to say, "Yeah, Henry really knows his stuff." Now that things have gone so well Carl takes some credit for the store's name: "Pets 'n' Stuff." Although I'm not sure it is deserved. I distinctly recall Carl suggesting "Helen Hens."

Anyway, it wasn't the name that brought the store to the attention of the Detroit buyers. Rather, it was the phenomenal success the German short-haired pointers from the store have had at various dog shows around the country. There was a five-year streak at the Gaines Field Trials that dogs from the store won top honors. And usually first and second runners-up, as well. The buyers or their experts theorized that pups raised as they were with all those stuffed birds develop a steadiness that borders on the inanimate. I mean to tell you these dogs can hold a point.

My personal opinion is that if a dog doesn't have a heart attack the first time it sees a bird rise in flight, it is definite championship material. It must be something for them to see a bird rise in flight the first time. Carl says, "Their steadiness comes from a 'mounting awareness' of their own mortality." Which he also contends gives them their wonderful dispositions.

Somehow during the expansion of the franchises something has been lost. Several stores are in financial trouble. For one thing, not a single champion has come out of a Pets 'n' Stuff store for the last three years (coinciding with the year that the Fairchilds sold). This year's Gaines Trials are being viewed in the corporate offices as an acid test for the concept.

The board meetings have really been squabbling matches lately. Some have suggested getting rid of the taxidermy side of the business. Others were suggesting that there is a much bigger market for "show dogs" on the confirmation side rather than obedience side. Some suggest cutting back on expansion and focusing only on improving existing stores. As Carl says, "Lots of heat, not much light."

One fellow has gone so far as to accuse Helen and Henry of being a couple of sharpies who suckered them into investing in a worthless venture. Can you believe that, though; I mean every one of them knows that last winter the Fairchilds decided to treat themselves with a trip to Europe. Henry said winter was the best time to go because he didn't need to go all the way to France to see Americans. It was their first flight as I recall and Henry wasn't too keen on the idea of flying. Carl told him he was just like that big green parrot they have at the store, "a big talker but a poor flyer."

I'm not sure we'll ever know the half of all that went on. They rented a car in Paris, but they were three days getting out of the city. Helen was worn out hearing Henry say, "Well, this is a side of Paris your average tourist never sees." "It was a side your average Parisians never saw either," Helen thought to herself as she longed to be that "average tourist" Henry was describing.

I guess one day after lunch they walked into a store. Helen wanted to do a little shopping, hoping she might find a nice winter coat. She was taking things off the racks and trying them on. No one in the shop spoke English (after all this was a side of Paris your average tourist ...). It was obvious the shopkeeper was agitated by the Fairchilds but there was no communication. Finally someone from the store went next door and returned with a person who spoke English.

You can imagine Henry and Helen's embarrassment when they found out they were in a dry cleaner's store. Henry feels there ought to be one of those universal symbols for dry cleaners. At any rate, my point is the Fairchilds aren't sharpies out to take anyone in.

At the board meeting last Wednesday, they finally decided to focus less on breeding champion bird dogs and get more involved in breeding well-dispositioned dogs and cats. That was really the Fairchilds' speciality all along, dogs and cats that love to be around people. Actually, that's a lot harder than championship dogs, show dogs, or taxidermy. And a whole lot less glamorous or profitable.

42

Well, I'd better get this in the mail before Mr. Hurley, the mail carrier, gets here. We're praying for you and your congregation.

Love to all,
Elizabeth

Pure in heart/Beatitudes
Blessed are the pure in heart, for they shall see God. (Matthew 5:8)

Dear Mike,

Well, church got out late on Sunday. I didn't get too much out of the last half of the sermon. I suppose we wouldn't complain so about Reverend Answers' delivery if he had anything to deliver. But if the truth be known, we were all still a bit groggy from Thanksgiving.

Carl says, "The turkey is the only one not hungry on Thanksgiving Day — he's stuffed." And "Coralie stuffs the turkey in the morning and the family in the afternoon."

The way some families around here cook, I suspect they're still serving leftovers from last year's Thanksgiving.

I suppose you recall how the day after Thanksgiving most people around here try to get their Christmas decorations up.

Many people were out but not for too long as it was the coldest day so far this winter. Carl said that it was so cold that everyone was using a four-letter word to describe it — Brrr! WOPE Radio had it exactly right when it forecast cold for the day. As a rule their forecasts are: partly cloudy, partly sunny, partly accurate.

Over at the Wilsons, Cheryl had been outvoted 3 to 1 by John and the boys on whether or not to hang decorations outside this year. The men of the house had opted instead for roof-mounting a Westar-Telecom Bobcat — an eighteen-inch satellite dish.

Cheryl had been against it from the beginning, arguing that 128 channels could only mean one thing — more television watching. John and the boys countered with it wouldn't be more television, just better. "Quality over quantity," was their battle cry.

"You know, Mom, more educational choices, CNN, a window on the world," was Matt's tack.

Mike took the position that Cheryl might find some programs of interest to her.

"Right," she countered, "when I have nothing to do, I can watch people doing nothing."

Last Wednesday, John and the boys drove over to Lansing and purchased the satellite dish and roof-mounting kit.

"It'll be an early Christmas gift the whole family can enjoy," John reasoned with Cheryl. "And you know how much Mom and Dad enjoy Lawrence Welk, and he's not carried on any of our local stations anymore."

The thought of her in-laws, whom she truly loves, coming over Saturday nights to watch Lawrence Welk was more than she could bear.

"We'll discuss programming choices later," she said icily, her mood matching the weather very closely. John went up on the roof with the mounting bracket and bolts. He got it all positioned and installed. Matt had gone up into the attic to assist by fastening the nuts onto the bolts from underneath.

John came back down from the roof half frozen with the wind blowing from the northwest and him working on the west side of the roof.

"I'll finish assembling this in the kitchen and then carry it up and snap it into place," he thought to himself.

It seemed like a good plan. However, if he'd taken the time to study the instructions, especially the parts in bold capital letters, he would have realized there was a sequence to the assembly that had to be followed. John would not discover this until it was too late.

"Who needs instructions? I'll use them if I get into trouble," was John's thinking on the value of instruction manuals in general.

After struggling for fifteen minutes up on the roof in subzero weather, he was beginning to think a peek at the installation booklet wouldn't be a bad idea. He had the dish properly mounted on the shaft, but for some reason the shaft wouldn't drop into the mounting bracket.

Like many do-it-yourselfers, John's last resort to making things fit together was a bigger hammer. By crimping the bottom of the shaft he'd gotten it partially started in the mounting box. But it wouldn't drop deep enough to allow tightening of the set screws.

Unfortunately, the bigger hammer John decided to use was himself. He figured if he sat in the dish his weight would force the whole thing together.

Cheryl was in the kitchen cleaning up the lunch dishes when she heard the commotion overhead. The snapping of metal and the grating of something across the roof and the plaintive wail of her husband alerted her to look out the kitchen window.

She was treated to the view of her husband sailing through the air seated on what looked like a mesh flying saucer, his hands blue from the cold, gripping for dear life. Did she imagine a Doppler effect in his scream as he sailed by? *Well, there goes Lawrence Welk and the Champagne Music Makers.* "Sank you, Boys," she thought to herself.

Cheryl, standing as she was, transfixed at the window, hardly noticed her boys racing out the back door to help their father up.

It could not be said that the satellite dish had broken John's fall. It, however, was broken. John, fortunately, had not broken anything, but had bruised himself in such a way that he won't be sitting down to enjoy television, even without satellite, for some time.

Carl said Sunday he could understand why they call them satellite *dishes* — "They're hard to fix and easy to break."

John has since been able to figure out that the dish's shaft slipped up through the mount before it is bolted in place. Maybe he should have looked at the instruction booklet. But for the time being, they have no plans for buying another.

John has been saying, "It cost me more to fly ten feet than it did for the Wright brothers to fly 200."

Well, I'd better get this in the mail before Mr. Hurley, the mail carrier, gets here. We're praying for you and your church.

Love to all,
Elizabeth

Advice
Listen to advice and accept instruction, that you may gain wisdom for the future. (Proverbs 19:20)

Dear Mike,

Well, church got out late on Sunday. I didn't get too much out of the last half of the sermon. Reverend Answers' shortcoming is longstaying. The sermon was what Carl refers to as, "Hither, thither and yawn." I believe Reverend Answers could talk forever on the value of silence.

Our weather took a sudden turn downward last week. At least the thermometer was down. Wally at WOPE Radio said there was no weather to report. The bulletin he read said, "Temperature at zero." We have had some snow already. I noticed a few kids making and throwing snowballs up onto their roofs and watching them roll back down somewhat larger with each toss as I drove in to the Busy-Bee Café last Thursday.

With the weather cooperating, it's easy to get into the mood for Christmas. And I doubt if anyone has more expectation each year than Blaine Richardson. Of course, he has time on his hands as the Refrigerator Magnet Museum slows down during the winter and is only open three days a week.

Ten years ago, Blaine had too much time on his hands at Christmas, also. But then he was "between jobs," which was almost a permanent state for him in those days. In fact, his brother, Blair, carried Blaine and Carolyn financially, off and on during those days.

Blaine had saved all of forty dollars to shop for Carolyn and their daughter, Lisa. He'd done a pretty good job, he thought, shopping for Lisa, but then she was only two and a half.

The Thursday before Christmas found him in Mayor's Jewelers at the mall in Lansing looking for something for Carolyn. The small windows that have the displays of rings, watches, and necklaces just glitter, and Blaine was like a moth to a flame. "They sure make it hard for a fellow with a $20 limit," he thought to himself.

He decided maybe jewelry wasn't the best idea and thought he'd look at some of the other stores. He was, after all, in no rush.

But rushing was what was going on in one of the offices downtown where one of the partners had just summoned a secretary to his office.

"Julie, I'd like for you to run over to the mall and get something for my wife for Christmas," he said.

"Something nice; you know what women like, something pretty, spangly." He felt rather proud of himself for coining a new word. "Keep it under a thousand dollars, and do it on your lunch hour. And get yourself something, too."

Julie had just about decided to quit after Christmas, but this was it! She would resign at the end of the year.

As Julie neared the entrance to Mayor's she noticed Blaine mesmerized at the small display window. "I wonder what he has his eye on?" she thought to herself. He was looking at a necklace with emeralds and small diamonds. It was beautiful and $900!

Blaine went back into the store resolute in his decision on getting a necklace for Carolyn. But with the thought in mind that the only thing harder than diamonds was monthly payments, he didn't see what he could do.

Julie had pretty well decided on the necklace in the window, unless Blaine was going to buy it. After all, he saw it first and it obviously would mean a lot more to him than her boss. And that's how it was that she began to eavesdrop on the conversation between the salesclerk and Blaine.

Blaine settled on a nice costume jewelry necklace. Julie bought the one in the window.

"The gift wrapping is free," said the clerk to Blaine.

"Please."

Julie had her boss' purchase gift-wrapped, too: same paper, same size box, same ribbon and bow.

In fact, the sameness was so striking that the security cameras would not even pick up the switch, nor who made it, nor if it was intentional. The two shoppers left the store at the same time. Both more or less satisfied with their afternoon at the mall.

On Christmas morning Blaine gave Carolyn the gift.

"I wish it could have been more," he said handing it to her, "You deserve better."

"Oh, Blaine, how did you ever?" she enthused as she held it up to look at it. "It's perfect! It's beautiful! It's wonderful!"

If Carolyn was surprised, Blaine was doubly so. His eyes just about popped out of his head. (We have no record of Julie's boss' wife's response, whose eyes may have also popped.) He suspected in turn, his brother, his mother, even Carolyn, of making the switch. *But how'd they know it was* that *necklace?* he thought. It couldn't have been any of them. It most surely was a miracle.

Like every good miracle, though, Blaine found he wasn't in a position to tell anyone about it. After all, you can't say to your wife, "Honey, that isn't the necklace I bought you. Mine was cheap and not real gemstones." So Blaine has carried a secret to the holiday each year. And that secret lends an air of expectation to Christmas that few others in town experience.

The next year, and, in fact, all the following Christmases, Blaine has been more interested in watching Carolyn open her gift from him than anything else under the tree. After all, who knows what she might find. In each successive year, he's been able to afford a better gift than the year before and I guess, if truth be told, he could probably afford a $900 necklace this year. But he's been thinking of maybe putting a $20 gift under the tree this year. Just to prime the pump. But this year, they don't need a miracle.

Well, I'd better get this in the mail before Mr. Hurley, the mail carrier, gets here. We're praying for you and your congregation.

Love to all,
Elizabeth

Miracles
He does great things and unsearchable, marvelous things without number. (Job 5:9)

Section 2:
Four Years Ago

Dear Mike,

Well, church got out late on Sunday. I didn't get too much out of the last half of the sermon. I was hoping for a message on New Year's abundance — and got last year's redundance. But if the truth be known, my mind was back at Christmas Eve's living nativity.

You recall how the youth and the Sunday school rotate year-to-year on who does the living nativity outside the church on Christmas Eve? This year, the Sunday school had the honors. The major effort goes into finding all the livestock and building a stable scene out of hay bales. The kids pretty well know their parts from previous years. I guess this year they had a donkey, a cow with her calf, several sheep, a couple of 4-H rabbits, and the one controversial guest — a potbellied pig. He's a cute little fellow named Beau by his owner, eleven-year-old Danny Olson.

Two years ago at the living nativity Danny was one of the shepherds, and he decided on the spot he had to have a sheep. His parents, Leonard and Janette, were able, after lengthy discussions, to convince him a sheep was a farm animal and inasmuch as they lived in town it was out of the question. But Danny wasn't to be denied — at least getting a pet.

Last spring he took his money into Helen and Henry's store, Pets 'n' Stuff, and purchased a potbellied pig.

If I remember correctly, it was one of the last sales they made before turning the store over to their daughter and son-in-law. I think you'll remember how they sold the concept to investors a few years ago and kept the original store here in town. They'd been talking for years about wintering in Florida. The winters were getting hard on Helen's arthritis, and Henry loves to fish and wanted to put some of his taxidermy skills to work on some deep sea fish. What is it Carl says? "Henry can mount any animal except a horse."

So they moved to Boca Raton earlier this fall. They bought a condo on the ocean in a gated community and settled in for a well-deserved retirement. But things didn't go so well. They didn't fit in with the neighbors, who, according to Henry, were "homeless." Some were home less than others, but all were home less than Helen and Henry, which meant, if Henry wanted to fish, he had to do it alone. And although they shared an interest in pets with many of their neighbors, it was more difficult to find people in Boca Raton who wanted to talk taxidermy. People wanted to talk, but mostly about themselves, "Hurricane season isn't the only time the wind blows in Florida," Henry would later say. The fishing wasn't really that good, either.

The clincher came after Thanksgiving when the homeowners' association asked them to repaint their van, which was the one they had used at the store. "Pets 'n' Stuff" was emblazoned on the side. Evidently, it broke at least one of the association's restrictions and covenants.

"I'm going home for Christmas," Henry told Helen at breakfast the Sunday before Christmas.

"I don't know what condition the house will be in. Should we call Karen and stay with them for the first few days?" Helen asked, somewhat relieved that they'd be home for Christmas.

They drove straight through and showed up at church just in time for the trouble.

Ernest Porter went through the roof when he saw the potbellied pig in the nativity scene. Immediately, he marched over to where Reverend Answers was standing. By his gait you could tell he was on a mission.

"What's the meaning of that pig up there?" Ernest demanded.

It was the first Reverend Answers had noticed Beau. It's easy for pastors to get distracted this time of year, as I'm sure you know. In fact, Reverend Answers had thought Beau was a dog, albeit not a particularly handsome one.

Before he could formulate a response, Ernest was on him.

"Pastor, that ain't biblical. You know there weren't any pigs at Jesus' birth," Ernest said heatedly.

"At least not a potbellied one," Reverend Answers replied, trying to defuse the situation with humor.

"You're not taking this seriously. Get that pig out of there," Ernest's voice was rising above the choirs of angels. "That pig is ruining Christmas — for all of us."

Ernest's one gift is his ability to rock the boat and convince everybody there's a terrible storm at sea.

Helen, who observed this with more than a little interest, looked at Henry. He had tears in his eyes.

"You don't mean you missed this, do you?" she asked.

"Just the opposite; this I can live without. I can't believe we drove two days straight to get here," he told her quietly. "But here we are."

Ernest was in Reverend Answers' face after the service. "I want the bishop's phone number so I can call him about this."

"The bishop's out of the area for the holidays," Reverend Answers answered dejectedly. "He's in Florida — Boca Raton, I think."

Helen and Henry were surprised that there was a gift for them under the tree at church — a refrigerator magnet Danny had made at school with his picture with Beau on it.

Ernest, pouring out righteous indignation and not knowing when to say "When," missed seeing his newly returned neighbors at church Christmas Eve. He went home before the gifts were passed out. In fact, it wasn't until Saturday at the Busy-Bee Café that he ran into them.

"What brings you folks back to town — the weather?" Ernest tried to joke.

"No, we missed the smallness," Henry said with (no small) irony.

"Did you hear how they tried to ruin Christmas?" he continued, not hearing what Henry had said. "They tried to put a pig in the manger. Some people will just ruin things if you don't watch them."

"And some will if you do," Helen joined in.

Well, I'd better get this in the mail before Mr. Hurley, the mail carrier, gets here. We're praying for you and that congregation.

Love to all,
Elizabeth

Acceptance
Letter of law
Spirit of law
When the Pharisees saw it, they said to him, "Look, your disciples are doing what is not lawful to do on the sabbath." (Matthew 12:2)

Dear Mike,

Well, church got out late on Sunday. I didn't get too much out of the last half of the sermon. Someone asked if Reverend Answers was long-winded. "Long but never winded," is what Carl answered. Of course, that may be changing. The new sign out in front of the church has a new message, "Sermons delivered hot in thirty minutes or less, or your money back." Carl says we'll be broke before the year is over.

We sure have had a winter to remember. The cold has disrupted everything. Schools have been closed, meetings cancelled, and several high school basketball games have had to be rescheduled. Why it's even been too cold for ice fishing. And if that isn't surprising enough, you'll know just what I mean when I say that the Thursday night pinochle and euchre card game at Gallagher's has even been affected. Now Mike, you can remember winter nights so cold that cars wouldn't start and those old men would come into town by snowmobile. Rudy called 911 for a ride, figuring he'd get out as they passed Gallagher's and Wally rode one of his Belgians and then was so worried that the horse might freeze to death that he talked Pat Gallagher into letting him bring the horse into the bar.

"Okay, but we don't serve horses in this bar," agreed Pat.

"That's why he brought his own," said Carl.

I guess that game has been going on for forty years or more. No one can remember when it didn't exist. It's a regular institution. What is it Carl says? "Rarely does a card player reach the pinochle of fame," or "A good deal depends upon luck and luck depends upon a good deal." It's amazing they let Carl in there as he usually just *talks* cards.

Two weeks ago Thursday the weather actually looked pretty good for a change. The sun was shining and a few things started to thaw out. Ray Vogel took it as a good omen for a night of cards and conversation. Ray has never been good at reading omens. That was not going to change. Nor was the trouble he's been having with his son-in-law. It is beyond him how Nancy could have married that boy, much less why Marcia insists on inviting them over for dinner so often.

If Ray looked forward to getting to Gallagher's, he was disappointed when he got there.

"Where is everybody?" he asked Pat.

"Well, Carl is in Florida, Jimmie's working nights again, and I heard a couple ewes lambed early at the Austins' farm. I suppose others will be along directly."

Ray sat at the bar and waited ... and poured out his troubles to Pat, who figured he had heard about everything by now. Ray's main problem was how little influence he has on daughter, Nancy, and son-in-law, Ryan. As he talked, he was surprised at how strong his feelings were. At one point he even teared up a little. Carl would have observed, had he been there, that Ray entered the tavern optimistically and had moved on to being misted optically.

"Well, the devil gives us our families," said Pat quoting some proverb he'd heard, "but thank God we get to pick our friends. Here's some change. Go feed the jukebox. Pick something to cheer yourself up."

Ray stared at the play list and wondered who had picked these songs. Eclectic would be a gentle way to describe it. Country western, classic rock and roll, show tunes, holiday music, and local artists would cover the main categories.

"Who picks what goes in here?" Ray asked, trying to make sense of a play list that he'd not paid much attention to until then, a list that included "Beer Barrel Polka," "I'm A Believer," and "Silver Bells."

"We cater to rather diverse musical tastes," Pat offered from behind the bar.

Before either had realized it, four hours had passed.

"I appreciate the company and hearing me out tonight," Ray said, putting on his mackinaw. "You want to unlock the door?"

"It's open, or it's supposed to be," Pat said, wondering if the lack of customers was somehow related to them being locked out.

58

It wasn't locked but it was sealed. Evidently, without the usual stream of patrons in and out, a ridge of ice had formed and welded the door shut.

"We'll have to call someone to come chip the ice away," Pat said.

"It's after midnight. Who we going to call? I'm not calling Marcia."

"Well, don't expect me to call her," said Pat. "How about your son-in-law?"

Each new suggestion seemed either too costly or way too embarrassing.

Finally Pat said, "We can sleep here tonight and get someone from the Busy-Bee to chip away the ice tomorrow morning."

"Sleep here, where?" Ray gasped as he imagined what had been spilt on the floor and tracked in. In fact, the floor now had the dry white film of tracked in salt.

"We'll bunk on the table," Pat said as he gestured with his head toward the shuffleboard table along the far wall.

It wasn't long until they'd stretched out under a couple table-cloths that had never, to the best of Ray's knowledge, even graced a table.

"It's not bad," Ray volunteered, "but the sand is getting in my clothes."

"Oh, don't worry, it'll turn into a pearl. Good night." Which was an amazingly accurate summary of the evening.

The blue light from the Stroh's clock even proved to be a fine night-light. The next morning they phoned Dwight at the Busy-Bee, and he and Rex came down before six and chipped them out.

Ray expected to have a fair amount of explaining when he got home. So he was somewhat surprised that Marcia had already explained it to herself, although incorrectly. She had imagined that having Ryan and Nancy over the night before had so upset Ray that he'd decided to stay out all night.

"We don't need to have the kids over for dinner as often," she ventured.

"What? No, that wasn't...." His voice trailing off as he figured out her take on his staying out all night.

"I'm okay with them coming over. I just need to add some songs to our juke box."

Fortunately, all Martha heard was, "I'm okay with them coming over." And his closing, "See what they're doing tonight," as he left the kitchen.

Well, I'd better get this in the mail before Mr. Hurley, the mail carrier, gets here. We're praying for you and that congregation.

Love to all,
Elizabeth

Mourning to dancing
Family
For "In him we live and move and have our being"; as even some of your own poets have said, "For we too are his offspring." (Acts 17:28)

Those who trouble their households will inherit wind. (Proverbs 11:29a)

I Borrowed
March 1

Dear Mike,

Well, church got out late on Sunday. I didn't get too much out of the last half of the sermon. Reverend Answers' sermon was straight from the shoulder, but I like it a little higher up. Speaking of a little higher up, Reverend Answers has a new hair cut. Carl says, "He gets it cut on Friday so he'll look good on the weak-end."

I did spend a little time Sunday morning planning my garden, which may have taken my mind off the message, too. The seed catalogues have arrived, the true harbinger of spring. But I suppose we'll have to wait another six weeks to get serious about putting out the gardens and setting up the cold frames.

I was in the Busy-Bee Café last Tuesday when Ernest Porter showed up. I think you know his personality well enough to agree when I say he's what the *Wall Street Journal* would describe as fiscally conservative. Around here we just say "tight." And I think it's fair to say his favorite Bible verse is, "Neither a borrower nor a lender be." Carl says, "He got his money the hoard way."

I remember a couple of years ago, at the Busy-Bee, Carl asked Ernest to loan him ten dollars. Ernest replied, "Lend a dollar, lose a friend." To which Carl replied, "Well, we're not really that good of friends."

So you can imagine the state Ernest was in when he arrived at the Busy-Bee Tuesday morning. He was waving a note in the air asking nobody and everybody, "Who's behind this?" His wife had found the note on their kitchen table when she returned from town a week ago Friday. It was a small, crumpled piece of "foolscap" written in pencil, most just illegible scratchings. But on closer inspection, about five words were legible: Ernest, I borrowed ... will return.... The rest was indecipherable. Including the most important thing, the signature.

When Martha showed Ernest the note, he couldn't really make sense out of it. Slowly he realized someone had stopped by while he was in one of the fields and Martha was in town — and horror of horror, had borrowed something. But what?

So the rest of Friday and all day Saturday and Sunday Ernest inventoried all his tools, a number of which at first turned up missing, but were later located where they'd been last used.

"Who would just come into our house and borrow something?" Ernest continually asked Martha. "I feel violated."

"Perhaps it's something from the kitchen, a cup of sugar or flour," she volunteered.

"Don't be ridiculous. The note's addressed to me."

Later he returned to the kitchen, asking Martha if there was anything missing. "I mean a mixer or the roaster?"

"How'd they get in, anyway? We always keep the place locked," he asked Martha, suspecting that she had forgotten to lock the door when she went to town. "I have half a mind to call the sheriff."

On Monday, the focus of the hunt shifted from the item borrowed to the borrower.

"Whose handwriting is this?" he asked his daughter, Joan, at the hardware store.

"I don't know. Sort of looks like Dr. McKnight's," she teased.

Ernest, not seeing the humor, asked, "Well, what would he want to borrow from me?"

By Monday night, half beside himself, it was dawning on him that perhaps he was the victim of a cruel hoax. And it was in that state that he showed up at the Busy-Bee Tuesday morning. He had a list of suspects drawn up, including, but not limited to, his neighbor Jim Hesler (motive but no opportunity), Carl (motive but no opportunity), his wife (opportunity, but where's the motive?), and about half of the town. So he went around the Busy-Bee asking everyone, "Have you ever seen this?"

By Sunday, I don't think Ernest was any closer to solving the mystery, but he and Martha were in church. Although, I don't think he got too much out of the last half of the sermon. He was too anxious waiting for a chance to look at the handwriting in the attendance pads for a match.

Well, here I've gone on too long about this and I don't want to give the impression that I'm the type that "writes others' wrongs." I better get this in the mail before Mr. Hurley, the mail carrier, gets here. We're praying for you and that congregation.

Love to all,
Elizabeth

Lending
Give to everyone who begs from you, and do not refuse anyone who wants to borrow from you. (Matthew 5:42)

... but the righteous are generous and keep giving. (Psalm 37:21b)

Dear Mike,

Well, church got out late on Sunday. I didn't get too much out of the last half of the sermon. The message was about Noah and the flood, and I couldn't help remembering how Carl says that Noah was the first person to preserve pairs. Actually, I didn't think this was a particularly good time of year to remind us of the weather, even if a flood isn't likely. We go to church to get our mind off our troubles, not be reminded of them. And the weather has been troubling us all for the past few weeks with way-below normal temperatures. March came in like a lion and stayed. We've had freezing rain, gale winds, and cloudy days. I could go on. The worst of it is that the sun has only been out about ten hours in the last two weeks. It was so bad that the one sunny day we did have, the Lansing paper's headline was "Prodigal Sun Returns." Wally, the weatherman at WOPE Radio, claims he has even had threats on his life.

You can tell it's getting to us by the way that people are acting. At the Busy-Bee Café people are just downright snappish. Darlene's tips are off by at least a third. What is it Carl says? "Darlene thinks tips grow on trays." Well, you can bet Darlene is in no mood to hear that.

Things aren't much better at Thelma's Cut 'n' Curl. You'll recall the sign in the window proudly proclaiming, "Where men are rare and the women are well done." You could say that when the conversation shifts from gossip to weather that the natural order has been upset. And that's just about all that they've talked about in the last three or four weeks.

Cheryl Wilson was thinking that a new hairstyle might cheer her up. And it did until she got home. Matt and Mike didn't even notice and when John got home he looked at her hair and said, "The wind must have really been blowing out there today."

Cheryl had already pretty much decided that she was going to take her aunt and uncle up on their offer for her to come spend a few days with them in sunny Lakeland, Florida. What she needed was a chance to thaw out, get away for a few days, and get some of that sun. Carl says the sun is the west's oldest settler.

So last Monday, John and the boys took Cheryl to the airport. As ornery as everyone has been, I think all were happy Cheryl was making the trip. Matt kept referring to this as the men's "Wild Man Week."

Surprisingly, things went pretty well for the boys and John. The boys took turns cleaning and John cooked. Well, there wasn't much cooking involved. Mike said it was "one canned thing after another." In fact, they were beginning to look forward to the school's "Tuna-Noodle-Hot-Dish," so Thursday the boys took over the meal planning and preparation. Matt stopped at Bradley's Market and bought calves' liver. Walt told him it was the easiest thing in the world to cook. And it did sound easy enough. Liver and onions is one of John's favorites, but Cheryl hates it and the smell, so he only has it at the Busy-Bee from time to time.

Matt chopped the two onions from the brown bag in the refrigerator to fry with the liver. He was surprised at how sweet they smelled. Almost perfume-like he thought. Of course, Cheryl will be surprised when she returns next Monday and discovers her two prize Christmas amaryllis bulbs missing.

John couldn't figure out exactly what was wrong with the liver, but he knew it wasn't quite right. But he went ahead and ate it. The flavor was strange, but not totally disagreeable. And after all, the boys had worked hard at fixing the meal. John suspected the onions were to blame and just didn't eat them. Of course, the boys hadn't realized until the liver was on their plates that they didn't like onions or liver, and since they had cooked it they didn't have to pretend.

It may have been a general queasiness induced by the bulbs or the lack of sunlight but by 8 o'clock they all were missing Cheryl. They called to see how she was doing. She'll be home next Monday and you can bet she'll bring along lots of warmth, if not pure sunshine.

I'd better get this in the mail before Mr. Hurley, the mail carrier, gets here. We're praying for you and that congregation.

Love to all,
Elizabeth

65

Knowledge

Teach me good judgment and knowledge for I believe in thy commandments. (Psalm 119:66)

Trust in the Lord with all your heart, and do not rely on your own insight. (Proverbs 3:5)

But grow in the grace and knowledge of our Lord and Savior Jesus Christ. To him be the glory both now and to the day of eternity. Amen. (2 Peter 3:18)

Dear Mike,

Well, church got out late on Sunday. I didn't get too much out of the last half of the sermon. But I'll take some of the responsibility because many Sundays I'm a mental tourist ... my mind wanders. As often as not, it wanders right out the front door of the church to some problem I'm experiencing. Last Sunday was a little different, though. At least my mind had wandered only as far as my garden.

It is looking pretty good so far this year, if I do say so. We've had plenty of rain and everything has greened up nicely. Right now the roses along the west side of the garden are in bloom. Their fragrance is so sweet it makes me linger in the garden, which helps with the weeding. You know what they say, "Tickle a garden with a hoe, and you'll harvest smiles."

I was in another garden Monday, Memorial Day. I like to put out some flowers around my parents' graves. The geraniums are doing well right now. Later this summer I'll put out some mums. Carl says they're appropriate for a cemetery. But then he says carnations are the Michigan state flower.

Actually, I was surprised to see Carl and Coralie at the cemetery Monday morning. Several people were there, but they all have relatives buried there and as far as I know Carl and Coralie don't. But they were sprucing up some untended graves.

I went over to ask if they were shopping or doing their community service. Coralie said a little of both. Carl said he was researching inscriptions on the tombstones, to which Coralie replied that she'd already written Carl's.

> *This stone to Carl was raised,*
> *Not so his jokes would be praised.*
> *For they are well known to all the town,*
> *But it was raised to keep him down.*

I wasn't aware of all that had been going on the last couple weeks at their house. Honduras, their dog, had gotten into some wasps or nettles or something that had raised a welt on his left front paw and his left hip. When he first limped home, they assumed he'd be over it in a day or two. And he probably would have if he could have left it alone. But you know how dogs are, they can't keep from licking and gnawing at a hot spot. After two days the place on Honduras's hip was getting bigger and rawer with each passing day.

I don't know if dog is man's best friend, although Carl is quick to point out that a dog never asks to borrow money, gives no advice, and has no in-laws. He'll say, "Honduras wags his tail not his tongue," and "He's not a pointer, he's a nudger; he's too polite to point." And so it goes. They need each other, although I'm not sure Carl is ready to admit it.

Well by the third day, Carl decided he and Honduras had had enough, but rather than "trouble the vet (Dr. Richardson)," which meant Carl didn't want to trouble his wallet, Carl went out to the garage and after a couple hours he had a makeshift collar for Honduras to wear. Carl had found an old belt and pop riveted a piece of stiff black plastic he'd cut from an old trash can.

The cone served its purpose; it prevented Honduras from licking his sore. Carl was full of himself. Of course they would soon enough find out that that wasn't all that the cone was preventing the dog from doing. Coralie said Honduras looked like the old RCA Victor dog who had gotten into the phonograph speaker and was peeping out with confusion rather than looking in with wonder.

I suppose every solution has its drawbacks. That night showed up a couple. First of all, Honduras couldn't fit out the dog door in the mudroom with the cone around his neck. In fact, he could barely turn around in there so he whimpered through the night. When he wasn't whimpering, he was pacing. Unfortunately, he, or should I say the cone, bumped into things, doorjambs, furniture, and the nightstand in Carl and Coralie's bedroom.

When Coralie heard the unmistakable sound of a porcelain music box shattering as it fell from the end table in the living room, she knew she'd had enough. Moments later Carl and Honduras knew it, too. It wasn't just a question of whether she'd put both Carl and his canine out, only which one was going first.

Well, Honduras went out and about twenty minutes later he was howling to get back in. And let me tell you, you haven't heard plaintive until you've heard that dog. That was the way it went all night, inside wanting out, and outside wanting in. And that was both Carl and Honduras.

Interestingly, things sort of settled down the next night. Carl had cut the cone down to where it was at least mathematically possible for it to fit through the trap door. But it was Honduras who had figured out how to use the door. (I tell you that is one smart pooch!) They had put Honduras out and were surprised in the morning to find him back inside.

Coralie discovered how he did it later in the day when Honduras backed into the mudroom from outside and then backed into the kitchen from the mudroom.

By the time I saw them on Memorial Day, Honduras was almost healed. Whether it was Carl's contraption, or Honduras losing interest in his sting, or the antibiotics Coralie had gotten from the vet that deserved the credit for the improvement was hard to tell.

Carl said, "We're thinking of getting plots here. The only question is whether we get one for Honduras or not. Coralie wants his headstone to read:

> *'Here lies Honduras, here let him lie.*
> *Now he's at rest, and so am I.'* "

I'd better get this in the mail before Mr. Hurley, the mail carrier, gets here. We're praying for you and your congregation.

Love to all,
Elizabeth

Memorial Day
Anxious/Worry
So do not worry about tomorrow, for tomorrow will bring worries of its own. Today's trouble is enough for today. (Matthew 6:34)

Dear Mike,

Well, church got out late on Sunday. I didn't get too much out of the last half of the sermon. Reverend Answers had what Carl calls an AT&T message: "Always Talking & Talking." The sermon read like a book, but unlike a book it couldn't be shut up. Actually, my mind was still on last weekend's "official opening" of the Refrigerator Magnet Museum for the season.

Memorial Day weekend marked the eleventh year of their being in business. What began almost as a protest against work by Blaine Richardson has certainly been through a fair number of changes. To say it has been something of a roller coaster ride for Blaine and his wife Carolyn would be an understatement. They have gone from struggling, to an overnight success, to the edge of bankruptcy, and back to solvency.

Over the years, the museum has not only grown but changed its direction somewhat. In the first couple of years it was just a museum of magnets, but with success came the need for a larger gift shop and, of course, a snack bar. Nowadays, the tourists end up spending more money and time with the latter two, than the displays themselves, which is something of a disappointment to Blaine. Then last year, word got out that the museum was a place of healing and comfort to arthritis sufferers.

I suppose in response to the influx of people who come and stay longer for the healing benefits of the magnets, Blaine decided to expand the snack bar into a full lunch service counter with the emphasis on healthy foods. It was natural to ask Rex from the Busy-Bee Café to come out for the summer and get him started. Rex seldom cooks lunch at the Busy-Bee as it is, so it seemed workable.

Rex went so far as moving his Airstream trailer out to the museum parking lot for the summer. His trailer has two large black stripes painted down the top, which gives it an uncanny resemblance to a toaster. (I'll have to tell you sometime how I know that.)

Blaine and Rex decided to call the food counter the "Garden of Eatin' " and focus on vegetarian dishes. I noticed earlier this spring that Carl must have had a hand in some of this as they had signs that read "We do dishes," and "Today's Special: You."

As I mentioned, Memorial Day weekend is something of a bellwether for the museum in terms of how the finances will flow this summer. So you can imagine Blaine's anxiety Saturday morning when he arrived at 6:00 to find a note from Rex taped to the door, reading "Sorry, had to dash to Indiana. Mother is sick." Blaine was feeling more than a little sick himself. Of all the things that go on at the museum, Blaine had to admit he knew the least about the food service.

When the Wilson boys, Matt and Mike, arrived at seven they advised Blaine to call Harriet Ornsley, the high school cafeteria head cook.

"She's got to be the only person around here who knows how to cook for several hundred people," Matt offered.

"I can remember her from when I was in high school," Blaine replied. "How old is she? Seventy?" he asked, answering his own question.

"She does live close and school's out for the summer," Mike continued.

"I don't know," Blaine worried. "She used to be awful bossy and what does she know about healthy cooking?"

"You have to admit she's a pretty regular customer. I mean I see her in here all summer," Matt said.

"Yeah, I think she comes for arthritis relief," Mike added.

"Does she still chew tobacco?" Blaine asked, resignation creeping into his voice as he called, and she agreed to be there in twenty minutes.

When Harriet arrived, she looked around. "Honey, you know what's wrong with this kitchen?" she asked Blaine as he gave her the tour. He knew she'd only asked the question so she could answer it. "You need more stuff," she added. "What's this white stuff in these boxes?" she asked Blaine, "Lard?"

"No, tofu," Blaine answered with just a note of superiority in his voice.

"Toe food?" she asked back.

"No, tofu."

"Honey, what kind of toes do they use?" she replied.

"Well, you've pretty well tied my hands on what I can do for you this weekend. Maybe I can get some stuff yet today from Bradley's. Will they deliver out here?" She was going a mile-a-minute. Blaine wasn't paying much attention, as he was trying to guess if she had a plug of tobacco in her cheek. "Today we'll offer grilled-cheese sandwiches and tomato soup," she continued.

I might have guessed, Blaine thought to himself.

Actually, Harriet brought a lot of creativity to the task. She figured the best way to get rid of all the tofu and yogurt was by blending up smoothies, which proved pretty bland until she came up with adding some honey and bananas.

On Sunday, she made up a peach smoothie with some Hale Haven peaches she'd canned last year and hadn't gotten around to using.

"This still is a little bland, don't you think?" she asked Blaine.

He had to admit that it was.

Blaine was afraid to get too far from the food counter for fear something terrible would happen if he didn't keep an eye on Harriet.

"Try it now," she said offering him a fresh smoothie as he cruised by.

"That's delicious!" he said, truly amazed at the transformation.

"What did you add to it?" Blaine asked uneasily eyeing a bottle of Peach Schnapps that was now resting near the blender.

"You know that Toe food blends up nicely; I'm thinking of trying a paté made of it and chicken livers."

"I'm not sure that fits our idea of healthy eating," Blaine began.

"Of course, we're going to need a couple more blenders, and you need to get the heavy duty ones."

Well, if nothing else, Blaine had his answer to one question. Yes, she was still bossy. Later in the day he was relieved to see her flambéing the Peach Schnapps in what Blaine took as more of an alcohol reducer than a flavor enhancer.

Monday evening Blaine was more than pleasantly surprised to see that the register tape from the Garden of Eatin' had more than doubled last year's income for those three days. He was also surprised when Harriet walked into his office without so much as a "by your leave," plopped down in the office's other chair, put her feet up on the desk, and announced the changes she had in mind for the gift shop.

"Blaine, you got a great thing going here, you just need someone like me to help you manage it."

"You might be right," Blaine relented. "You've certainly proved yourself in the kitchen."

"By the way," she interrupted, "you got anything I can spit in?"

Well, I'd better get this in the mail before Mr. Hurley, the mail carrier, gets here. We're praying for you and that congregation.

Love to all,
Elizabeth

Helping/Work/One another
Welcome one another, therefore, just as Christ has welcomed you, for the glory of God. (Romans 15:7)

Dear Mike,

Well, church got out late on Sunday. I didn't get too much out of the last half of the sermon. If you ask me, the recipe for a good sermon includes some shortening. Carl says Reverend Answers has the Midas touch in his preaching. "Everything he touches turns into a muffler."

I'm surprised Carl had any sense of humor after all that he's gone through the last couple of weeks. Hopefully, things are all cleared up now.

I first got wind of all of this just over a week ago at Thelma's Cut 'n' Curl. Dorothy was in the shop that morning asking if anyone knew how Carl and Coralie were getting along, which seemed like a strange question. I'll admit Dorothy is the type of person who loves to talk about things that leave her speechless. What is it Carl says? "She's got a great sense of rumor."

The whole shop is so bad about putting two and two together to equal scandal that Thelma has threatened to put up a sign saying: "Caution! The talk in here will curl your hair," and calling the Thursday morning customers, "The spies of life" and "Scandal prospectors."

Let me give you a little background on what started this latest incident.

Two weeks ago, Carl asked Coralie if she'd be interested in seeing an authority on diamonds, which Coralie knows from long experience meant a trip to Comerica Park to see a baseball game. This has become something of a midsummer's ritual for Carl, ever since the days of the old Tiger Stadium, and he was anxious to go and take another trip down memory lane. We've all heard Carl in the Busy-Bee say that if a man wants to see a baseball game in the worst way, he'll take his wife. So I'd guess this was pretty important to him.

Coralie doesn't really care for the game; she says there's too much bawl in baseball anymore, but she agreed to go along.

They drove down Thursday night two weeks ago, driving by their old parking spot on Church Street. Carl could remember parking there when it was someone's front yard and the charge was one dollar. And there was no way to leave early as the front yard was filled with cars.

Carl was pleased that they had been able to get pretty good seats along the third base line, and he settled in with a couple red hots (hot dogs) and a beer.

It was a cool night with the prospect of a hot game. As if that weren't enough, Carl and Coralie were seated next to a couple from Chapin. Although they didn't know each other, they knew enough people in common to keep the conversational ball rolling during the time between innings.

Coralie excused herself in the fifth inning to freshen up and that's when things got interesting.

Carl was quite pleased with his good fortune, as both the husband and wife enjoyed Carl's jokes. To their delight, Carl ran off his classic about baseball in the Bible. You may recall it: "In the big inning, Eve stole first, Adam stole second, Gideon rattled the pitchers, Goliath was put out by David, and the prodigal son made a home run."

Carl and Coralie weren't the only people from town at Comerica Park that night. Blair and Blaine Richardson were also in attendance.

You know how during the breaks in the game the cameras scan the crowd and project people on the Jumbotron? Well, as you might guess, the camera panned the third base line seats and slowed and stopped on Carl.

"Look up there!" Blair said excitedly to his brother. "Are you seeing what I'm seeing?"

"Is that Carl?" Blaine asked and in the same breath: "Is that Betty Richland?"

And then the image was replaced by some kids' faces.

"What are those two doing at a game together?" Blair asked no one.

"You don't suppose?" Blaine ventured.

The notion gnawed at both brothers the rest of the game. Both were sure they hadn't seen either Coralie or Betty's spouse in the picture that was on the Jumbotron.

"What kind of fool would cheat on his wife at a baseball game? I mean, anybody could see them," Blair opined.

"Someone who wanted to see the game in the worst way," ventured Blaine, trying to quote Carl.

Neither brother enjoyed the rest of the game, although Carl, Coralie, Betty, and Dick did. Carl told them after the game that he felt like a ball player himself as he was hoping they'd all get home safely.

Blair and Blaine decided they wouldn't tell anyone what they'd seen or suspected. Of course, the next day they'd proved nothing circulates as quickly as a secret. After all, when somebody asks if you can keep a secret, it's always someone who can't.

Four days later, when Coralie got her hair done, Thelma asked if she knew where Carl had been last Thursday.

"The Tiger baseball game," Coralie replied. "You know he had his heart set on going. Said it would make him feel young again."

"I'll bet it did," said Darlene, as she was hanging on every word.

"You know, for old time's sake," Coralie continued.

"And you approve?" Thelma asked incredulously.

"Don't get me wrong; I don't enjoy it," Coralie continued, "but it's better this way than Carl going with one of the guys."

Darlene swears Thelma swooned at that moment. Whatever happened in the ensuing commotion, a smattering of truth began to get out. So, I guess Carl's in the clear.

I'd better get this in the mail before Mr. Hurley, the mail carrier, gets here. We're praying for you and that congregation.

Love to all,
Elizabeth

Gossip

I tell you, on the day of judgment you will have to give an account for every careless word you utter. (Matthew 12:36)

... but no one can tame the tongue.... (James 3:8a)

Judgment

Let us therefore no longer pass judgment on one another, but resolve instead never to put a stumbling block or hindrance in the way of another. (Romans 14:13)

County Fair Ribbons
August 2

Dear Mike,

Well, church got out late on Sunday. I didn't get too much out of the last half of the sermon. Reverend Answers has that melodious voice. What is it Carl says? "It's a wind instrument" — and one does tend to drift during the sermon. I will say that he has kept busy with the new sign out in front of the church. Last week it said, "Be the soul support of your family."

The weather's been unusually hot the last couple of weeks. By sundown, it's usually pretty sticky. But the fireflies seem to make light of the situation.

Speaking of "making light," I wish I could make light of something that happened at this year's county fair. You know how much I enjoy the fair each year. Once again, this year I'd entered several things in the homemaking arts division. I was pretty sure my caramel sour cream cake would be a winner. Coralie says that cake is "a moment in the mouth, hours in the stomach, and years on the hips," so you know it's good. I've pretty well resigned myself to not getting a ribbon for my pickles or relish. That woman from Chapin is just unbeatable. But I did have some nice produce to show, too.

I'll never understand why it is that you put two seeds in the ground and one does so well and right beside it the other is not much to show for the effort. This summer I have had some luck with the melons. In fact, I don't know what surprised me more this year, the blue ribbons on the melons and squash or the blue ribbon on the bread and butter pickles. Of course, I was kind of counting on the blue ribbon for the cake, so that wasn't a surprise. Carl said it was the icing that put me over the top. But I gave him some of his own medicine; I said, "Icing is what I do in the shower."

When I saw the ribbon on my pickle jar, I was just about floating. I actually thought about framing it. Needless to say, after the judging I was in the mood to celebrate. I started on the midway with the roast corn booth. Carl says those who like that corn are "cobblers." I was on my way to the lemonade stand when I ran into a dejected looking Mike Wilson.

Mike and several other kids from the church are in the 4-H program and have projects they've been working on. A couple have raised steers and hogs and rabbits for the livestock competition. But mostly they've worked on projects. Mike had entered a couple of things in different divisions. He had a sure winner in dressmaking. His dress is what we'd all like to make. As Carl says, "One that makes the wearer look slim and all others look around." Cheryl will be modeling it at church one of these days. Actually, Carl has been teasing Mike a little about sewing. He'll say, "That Mike sure knows the seamy side of life," or "As you sew, so shall you rip."

I went back to the homemaking arts barn with Mike to see if I could see why he didn't get a ribbon. I was shocked. Some little old calico print dress had a blue ribbon. I mean everyone knows how much harder velvet is to sew and Mike's was done perfectly. The seams were meticulous. The dress had some flair and class.

I went looking for Clea Benson, who I knew was one of this year's judges.

"We couldn't let a boy win the blue ribbon. Think what it would do to his self-esteem."

I couldn't believe my ears — "do to *his* self-esteem," as if doing your best and losing because you're a boy is a boost to his self-esteem.

"Anyway, what's done is done," she continued. "The ribbons have been awarded."

"Are you telling me what my own two eyes already have? That Mike's dress was the best?" I asked with mounting anger, "And that someone else got the blue ribbon?"

"I didn't say his was best. I said, 'How would it look if a boy won?' I remember when ..." she trailed off, noticing the rather wild look in my eye. In fact, if I could have gotten to my cake I'd have thrown it at her. Carl says your temper is the only thing you can lose and still have.

As it was, I still had mine the next day when I wrote to Clea and the other judges saying I wouldn't be accepting any ribbons this year. I'll tell you it was hard to not keep the pickle ribbon, which is really the only one that mattered to me. But who knows, probably some man had entered some really first-rate ones and the judges had to protect him, too. I mean it's just not right.

Clea said she remembered when boys didn't even enter sewing and cooking projects. That is the problem, trying to "remember when" when we'd all be better off if we'd keep asking "What's new?"

Well, I'd better get this in the mail before Mr. Hurley, the mail carrier, gets here. We're praying for you and that congregation.

Love to all,
Elizabeth

Prejudice/Change
You must not distort justice; you must not show partiality; and you must not accept bribes.... (Deuteronomy 16:19a)

I am about to do a new thing; now it springs forth, do you not perceive it? (Isaiah 43:19a)

Signs
September 1

Dear Mike,

Well, church got out late on Sunday. I didn't get too much out of the last half of the sermon. Carl said, "It was loud, forceful, and clashed with everyone's sensibilities, and that was just Reverend Answers' tie." But if the truth be told, I was somewhat distracted by the heat.

I'm beginning to believe there's something to this global warming. This had been an unusually hot August, probably a record around here. It was made all the more unbearable by the lousy winter and spring we had. Every time we bring up adding cooling to the church it gets voted down as an impractical expense for no more than we'd use it. Reverend Answers says at least the church is "prayer conditioned."

But it was just steamy in church. In fact, when I went to Thelma's Cut 'n' Curl on Monday, she even commented on how my hair had lost its curl and suggested I needed a new permanent. Now if that isn't false advertising I don't know what is. I mean how permanent is it if I need a new one every couple of months? But I always enjoy getting my hair done.

Earlier this summer, she was telling me when she was younger she couldn't decide if she should become a hairdresser or a writer.

"How'd you decide?" I asked.

"Tossed a coin," she replied.

I thought for a moment, "Came up heads?"

"Right."

But she does have a way with words. You can tell that in the clever little signs she has up in the shop.

"We curl up and dye for you," "Dye now, gray later," and "If your hair isn't becoming to him you should becoming to us." And you'll remember the slogan from the pew fans, which, I might add, are getting a lot of use these days.

It's been a little hotter than is comfortable down at the Busy-Bee Café lately. And surprisingly, signs are behind the trouble.

Earlier this summer, Dwight got a little sign-happy, and started putting up signs, too. The "Open for Business" sign is still on the door, but in the window a sign reading, "No Reservations Needed" was a little pretentious, I guess, as everyone in town already knows this. Later, a sign appeared in the window saying, "No Shoes, No Shirt, No Service." I guess Dwight had found these signs for sale in one of the restaurant supply catalogues.

I suppose if it had stopped there, nothing untoward would have happened. But in July, he installed the signs in the restrooms, reading, "Employees are required by law to wash hands before returning to work." Since there are only two full-time employees, Darlene the waitress and Rex, who cooks when Dwight's wife Arlene is off, the two of them felt they'd somehow been singled out.

Rex stormed out of the café after heated words last week: "Either the signs go, or I go." He spent two days in his Airstream that's parked out at Lake Chemung. I assume he was trying to figure out what to do.

"You know, Darlene and I don't like the implication of those signs in the restrooms," he began with Dwight.

"What implication?" asked Dwight honestly.

"That we haven't been washing our hands."

"Well, it's the law," was Dwight's response.

"Is it the law that you have to put a sign up, too?" asked Rex, feeling his heat index rising.

"Anyway, the sign is for our customers. It makes them feel better," continued Dwight.

During the week, one could sense that the war was still raging, and Rex or Darlene or both had taken up a guerrilla campaign against all the signs but the handwritten one on the cash register that says, "A tipped waitress doesn't spill."

The first volley was a change on the "Open for Business" sign. Someone had put an H in front of Open to alter the sign to read "Hopen for Business." A day or two later, the "No Reservations Needed" saw the altering of the N to an H rendering the sign "No Reservations Heeded." Dwight wisely took down the "No Shoes, No Shirt, No Service" sign before one of the letters in it was removed.

Likewise, on the other front, the signs were disappearing from the restrooms, and just as fast Dwight would replace them with new ones. You can imagine how this affected business. I mean who wanted to eat in a combat zone?

I guess it was Arlene who finally drove Dwight back to the bargaining table.

"If you're not careful, Rex will just pack up his Airstream and move on," she reasoned.

"And I'll tell you, I'm not interested in cooking twelve hours a day anymore."

"Well, what am I going to do, it's the law!" Dwight whined.

"I'm sure you and Rex will work out something," she said.

I guess they compromised by Monday last week. After my stop at Thelma's, I noticed a couple of new signs. One I think Carl suggested months ago: "Oh, what foods these morsels be." But the most obvious change was in the restrooms. The sign now read, "Employees must wash one hand before returning to work." I believe this Zen approach was suggested by Darlene, who remained above most of the controversy.

The last couple of days, I think I've noticed a touch of fall in the air. And most of us have our minds on the Festival of the Water Tower, which is next weekend.

Well, I'd better get this in the mail before Mr. Hurley, the mail carrier, gets here. We're praying for you and that congregation.

Love to all,
Elizabeth

Compromise/Conflict
Remind them of this, and warn them before God that they are to avoid wrangling over words, which does no good but only ruins those who are listening. (2 Timothy 2:14)

Wisdom
The mind of the righteous ponders how to answer, but the mouth of the wicked pours out evil. (Proverbs 15:23)

Dear Mike,

Well, church got out late on Sunday. I didn't get too much out of the last half of the sermon. People weren't just looking at their watches — they were shaking them. Reverend Answers takes a text and preaches from it, usually far from it.

The fall has been unusually warm. I've been sitting out on the porch fascinated by the leaves by moonlight. We still haven't had a frost, although the leaves are starting to turn. It is a pretty drive into town along that stretch of Hollister Road where the trees form a canopy over the road. And in a couple weeks you'll think you're driving through a kaleidoscope.

Most of us have started to prepare things for the church's Harvest Bazaar and Fallfest. I'm putting up some pickles. The women's group has been working on mincemeat filling and a quilt to raffle off. Several of us will bring baked goods.

The Wilson boys came up to my house last week on a rather flattering mission. They had decided to make pumpkin pie filling to sell at the bazaar, and they were hoping I'd supply them with a recipe and a couple of large kettles.

I appreciate how each year they take time, usually a fair amount I might add, and work on something for the Fallfest. It was several years ago now that they worked on their first one. I remember they were given the task of painting the signboard in front of the church to say "Rummage Sale." Matt started at one end and Mike the other thinking it would be easier for both of them to work at once. I guess they'd gotten about half way when they took a break. When I drove up the sign read "Rum Sale." Which may have accounted for the unusual number of people who stopped by that year.

"Our idea," Mike began, "is to get a couple of the giant pumpkins that the Shepherds are raising and render them into pumpkin for pies."

"We'd like to use your recipe," Matt continued, "since it's the best we've ever tasted."

"Flattery will get you nowhere," I lied. "But I don't have any experience with those giant pumpkins," I continued in a more truthful vein.

In fact, I don't really think of them as pumpkins at all. A pumpkin shouldn't be raised for size, but for taste and color. My suspicions that they were mostly water and very little pumpkin proved to be amazingly accurate.

"We've already printed up some sample labels on the computer, and we'll put them on the jars," Matt said. I was impressed.

"Piety Pie Filling," read the label, with the subhead, "We're Putting the Pie in Piety."

Carl was later to say that he'd suggested "Piety Pie Filling," subheaded, "Let This Be Your First Taste of Religion."

The Shepherds were glad to have the Wilsons cart away some of the smaller giants, which I'd guess weighed in between 35 and 50 pounds. As I said, that's not a pumpkin, but then the price was right: free.

So last Saturday while John and Cheryl were out of town, Matt and Mike turned the family kitchen into a pumpkin production facility. With quart jars cleaned and ready to go, the boys began boiling the pumpkins down. They had cleaned and cubed the meat and settled down to some serious stirring as they had four big pans going on the stove at once.

The pumpkins being as they were at least 90% water, took a long time to boil down. But by late in the afternoon they had put up almost twenty quarts of pie filling and had them sealed, labeled, and crated for the bazaar. All the steam had made the kitchen feel like a sauna. Needless to say, they felt great in their exhaustion. They were pretty well done in by the time the last kettle was washed, dried, and put aside. So they did something I do every afternoon — they took a nap.

About 4:30 they were awakened from their naps by Cheryl's screams from the kitchen.

"What's happened in here?" she yelled. "Who did this? Oh, how could they?"

Matt and Mike turned the corner into the kitchen just in time to see Cheryl slump into one of the kitchen chairs. The second thing they noticed was how all the wallpaper had peeled off the wall.

Evidently, all the steam had loosened the paste in the kitchen and the weight of the wallpaper had just pulled itself off.

The boys spent Saturday and Sunday scraping paste off the walls. Cheryl hasn't decided if she's going to paint it or if the boys will be "putting up" another delicacy — wallpaper.

I should say that I did sample a quart of their pumpkin filling. It wasn't bad. However, I'll stick with my original judgment. The emphasis is on size, not taste. But I'm proud of the boys for trying. What is it Carl says? "People who are generous seldom go crazy; of course, it's another matter for those who live with them."

I made two pies with the quart I got, one of which I took to the Wilsons. It was well received, even by Cheryl, and you will recall she was grieving. But I believe it lifted everyone's spirits. It did mine to make it and to give it. If I can add my two cents, I'd say, "There is a little pie in the hap-*pie*-st." And I'm thankful for that.

Well, I'd better get this in the mail before Mr. Hurley, the mail carrier, gets here. We're praying for you and that congregation.

Love to all,
Elizabeth

Generosity
... for during a severe ordeal of affliction, their abundant joy and their extreme poverty have overflowed in a wealth of generosity on their part. (2 Corinthians 8:2)

Dear Mike,

Well, church got out late on Sunday. I didn't get too much out of the last half of the sermon. I will say Reverend Answers does have a unique ability, though. He's the only man in town who can keep dozens of women quiet for a half-hour. And who am I to complain? The sermon was refreshing. At least I always feel refreshed after a nap.

I doubt if I was the only one whose mind was more on last Friday's homecoming game than on the sermon. The weather was very good — clear and crisp. The moon was up in the sky. What was it Carl said? "The moon is silvery because it makes change in quarters." Now some years the weather is downright dismal, but it fails to keep many people away. One year it rained so hard that it was more a *drownpour* than a downpour. Carl said, "Rain is the only thing that comes down — and even then it soaks you."

We've always had good football teams here. I think you'll recall some of the teams from your time here. Carl says our wins are because we have a coach pulled by charley horses. No doubt, Coach Olson has done a great job with the boys. And the boys work hard physically.

But I think there might be some more plausible explanations for our teams' successes. Down at the Busy-Bee Café, I've heard people express the opinion that it's our loyal fans. What is it Carl says? "The football players do the running and the spectators do the kicking." This town does support the players. I think that was one of the reasons we were selected to be an Olympic training site again this year.

The school booster club still buys the letter jackets for all the kids. Ed Reddman and Sons has stayed in business selling the jackets and related sports gear. I know Rick, Ed's son, still takes great pride in fitting each girl or boy with a jacket.

Cheryl told me when she took Matt down a couple years ago it was a joy for her and Matt. Rick always makes a great show of measuring each young customer, then proceeds to recommend a jacket one or two sizes larger. There is a method to his madness, and in fact, I think it underlies the real reason for the team's successes over the years.

Of course, Rick tells the athlete and parents, "You want a little extra room in case you want to wear a sweater under it on the coldest days," which is true enough.

But isn't there an even subtler message here? "You're not finished growing." And in fact, that's true for most all of our kids.

All the jackets are given out at the pep assembly Friday before homecoming. That way all the kids who are getting jackets get them in time to wear them to the homecoming game. Over the years, there have been a few mix-ups — with a jacket or two getting to the wrong person.

The letter jackets have changed over the years. I guess the biggest change is that the girls now can earn their jackets on the sports field. And to accommodate the change, Reddman and Sons no longer bills itself as the complete store for dads and lads. Years ago the name was Reddman and Sons Haberdashery. Carl said that meant a store for men whose wives didn't pick their clothes. Now, of course, they carry clothes for everyone.

A few years ago, the jacket sleeves went from fabric to leather. But the colors have stayed the same: burgundy and gray. Gray sleeves and burgundy body. Each student's full name is embroidered on the inside and first name on the left breast pocket area. And across the back the words: "Maybe Champions."

You know the team was named Champions in the sense of a defender of a cause or the rights of others, although no one is disappointed when the teams are also victors, which, as I mention, has been the case more often than not during the years. And nowhere more so than on the football field.

So, of course, we were a bit more concerned than usual this year with the team three and three going into Friday's homecoming game against Chapin.

Carl opines, "Football, not baseball, is our national pass time," and "Football must be the cleanest sport. After all, it has scrub teams!"

Well, with all the freshly minted letter jackets we did look clean. It's fun to see the kids walking around in jackets two sizes or so too big. Some of the men in town still wear their jackets to the games, or at least to homecoming. Their jackets are now that "perfect fit." They've all grown one way or another to fill out the jacket, some across the chest, some a little lower. But it is a source of pride, just like a wife who can still fit into her wedding dress. All in all, it was a wonderful homecoming. Good to see the town's support, the team on the field, the new jackets, the pre-leather ones, the new ones, and the Maybe Champions.

Well, I'd better get this in the mail before Mr. Hurley, the mail carrier, gets here. We're praying for you and that congregation.

Love to all,
Elizabeth

Growth/Maturity/Sanctification
But speaking the truth in love, we must grow up in every way into him who is the head, into Christ. (Ephesians 4:15)

But grow in the grace and knowledge of our Lord and Savior Jesus Christ. To him be the glory both now and to the day of eternity. Amen. (2 Peter 3:18)

Champion
The Lord your God, who goes before you, is the one who will fight for you, just as he did for you in Egypt before your very eyes. (Deuteronomy 1:30)

89

Frozen Car Door
December 5

Dear Mike,

Well, church got out late on Sunday. I didn't get too much out of the last half of the sermon. It was a "rocking chair sermon"; back and forth, but not much progress. I've just about decided the only way to stay awake during the sermon is to give it. If the truth be told, I suppose I was still a little sluggish from Thanksgiving. By Sunday, all traces of Thanksgiving dinner were gone from the refrigerator, and that's saying a mouthful.

We're enjoying the mildest fall on record, as temperatures are still in the 60s. My garden is still producing some chard and squash, this after one of the harshest springs in recent memory. Usually by this time of year I'm only turning it over in my mind. What is it Carl says? "Gardening is a painstaking endeavor, especially in the small of the back."

Wally, WOPE's weatherman, has just about given up trying to predict the weather. Most mornings he just says, "The weather is unsettled."

It was unsettled two weeks ago Saturday. Matt Wilson was looking forward to his first date with Leia Axner. He'd invited her to the school's homecoming dance. It had taken him since early September to get ready for the date. Well, six weeks to work up the nerve to call her and one week to worry about what to wear.

Cheryl suggested asking his grandfather, George, if he could borrow his new Cadillac. I doubt if Matt would have had the courage to do it if she hadn't made the suggestion. The '99 Sedan DeVille is George's pride and joy.

"Grandpa, I was wondering if I might borrow your car for a date this coming Saturday?" Matt asked.

"Where you want to go? With whom? What time will you need it? When will you have it back?" George fired off in rapid succession, not waiting for a full answer.

Matt played up how he wanted to make a good first impression.

"I don't know, Matt, driving a Cadillac might be loving beyond your means," George offered in jest.

"Didn't you want to make a good impression when you were dating Grandma? Did you ever take her to a dance?" Matt asked.

"Oh, sure, we used to have barn dances when I was your age. I took your grandma to a barn dance several times, but all I got from her was the same old stall."

Matt knew he had the car when George started trying to make jokes.

"One last thing, if you want to use it, you'll have to wash it. And don't forget to use the Club when you lock it up!"

Matt picked up the car at 4:00, took it home and washed it up, then went inside and dressed up. By then it was looking like we'd get our first hard freeze of the winter. I remember I was out in the garden trying to cover up a few plants when Matt drove by around 5:30.

As night fell, so did the thermometer. In fact, it was in the 20s when Matt pulled up at Leia's house. Matt was surprised to find that his door wouldn't unlock. "Let me try the passenger door," he said to himself. It wouldn't budge, either. He reached around back to the back doors and found the same. All four doors, actually the locks, had frozen from the wash water on the drive over.

Leia and her family had noticed the headlights when Matt pulled into the drive and were wondering what was taking him so long.

Meanwhile, Matt was finding out the Cadillac's windows were frozen shut, too, or at least the motor arms. He decided to honk the horn.

Leia was about to leave when her father said, "No daughter of mine is going out with a boy who won't come to the door and meet her parents."

Leia sat uneasily in the big chintz-covered chair. "Unsettled" just about covered the mood in the Axner living room. The honking continued.

Neither Leia nor her parents were familiar enough with Morse code to realize he was doing 3 short, 3 long, 3 short. Matt's eye kept going to the Club. What would a broken window cost compared to a broken heart? (Of course, his grandfather's heart was the one in question.)

Matt had just about decided to drive home and get some help when he lit on another plan. If it was unsettled in the house, it was hot and humid in the car. He turned the heater up full blast and started throwing his shoulder into the door as he tried to open it. In ten minutes, Matt had taken off his leather jacket, wool sweater, and shirt. He was sweating profusely, still occasionally tapping out SOS on the horn and beginning to wonder what kind of family Leia was from. He was sure he'd seen her father walk past the picture window at least ten times and look out at him. Jim Axner was sharing a similar train of thought, wondering about what kind of family Matt was from.

The heat finally did the trick on one of the windows. Matt climbed out in his T-shirt and stocking feet. He was afraid to step on the leather seats.

Jim was embarrassed when he heard Matt's story of being trapped in the car. Here he'd imagined the worst about Matt. To make amends he insisted Leia and Matt drive his almost brand new F-150 pickup. And Jim volunteered to try to warm up and dry out the doors and locks with a hairdryer and space heater.

Matt retrieved his shoes and clothes from the Cadillac and looked a lot more presentable as he eased the new truck out of the driveway. The dance turned out great. Matt and Leia hit it off.

The ride home was great. It was cold enough for Leia to sit close to Matt.

"I was afraid you weren't going to come in," Leia volunteered as the truck pulled into the driveway, "and that you'd just drive away when I didn't come out to the car."

"I was worried I'd have to go home and tell my grandfather I broke his car," Matt said as he eased the truck into the parking spot. "I'd better go in and thank your father."

"Well, he needed to lend you the pickup after making you sweat out there for fifteen minutes," Leia answered.

"Actually, I want to thank him for letting you go out with me after all the honking," Matt said.

Carl says, "Love is when two people close their eyes and can see heaven." You know, I think Matt and Leia got a glimpse that night.

Well, I'd better get this in the mail before Mr. Hurley, the mail carrier, gets here. We're praying for you and that congregation.

Love to all,
Elizabeth

Understanding
... seeing they do not perceive, and hearing they do not listen, nor do they understand. (Matthew 13:13b)

Love
Love is patient; love is kind; love is not envious or boastful or arrogant.... (1 Corinthians 13:4)

Section 3:
Three Years Ago

A Bonus
January 1

Dear Mike,

Well, church got out late on Sunday. I didn't get too much out of the last half of the sermon. What is it Carl says? "Preachers, unlike guns, the smaller the caliber, the bigger the bore." The sermon was what I'd term a Vincent Van Gogh sermon. I listened with one ear.

I think most of us were either thinking about Christmas or looking ahead to the next year. Christmas was wonderful here. It was cold and there was lots of snow, although Wally, the weatherman at WOPE Radio, missed the call about the snow. I'm pretty sure that the station is missing one piece of scientific equipment that would make the predictions more accurate: a window. He is predicting a blizzard with power outages for this new year.

Carl always says this is the time of year when "we exchange hellos with strangers and good buys with friends." There is a spirit of generosity and good will that is hard to find at other times of year.

I guess it was that spirit that drove Blaine Richards to his brother Blair's two weeks before Christmas. I think I wrote how Blaine has a tradition of giving all the Refrigerator Magnet Museum employees a Christmas bonus, and that this year business hadn't been good enough to generate the profits to support that generosity.

"Let me see if I understand what you're asking for," Blair said after hearing Blaine's request. "You want to borrow $1,500 to give to the people who work for you."

"Well, it's Christmas, and I'd like to do a little something for them," Blaine continued.

"Why don't you give them a bonus based on performance? I was just reading an article last week saying that all the top companies were tying the employees' bonuses to performance," Blaine got going. "In fact, if you got a little more work out of some of those people, you wouldn't be sitting here asking me for a loan."

Blaine couldn't help recalling two of Carl's classic statements: "The easiest way to be left alone is to ask for a loan," and "The only thing you can get at Christmas without money is depressed."

"Do you think you can help out or not?" Blaine said, moving the lecture along. "You know Mom will loan it to me," he continued, playing his trump card.

"She can't afford it, but you're right, she'd give it to you." Blaine sighed, getting up from the kitchen table to look for his checkbook.

Blaine had an easier time with his mother, hitting her up for a $500 loan.

Now I won't say Blaine saved Christmas, but I know most of the employees were surprised and elated with their bonuses, as they all knew financially this had not been a good year for Blaine or the museum.

About the same time as Blaine was approaching Blair for a loan, Jim Hesler had decided he'd send Ernest Porter a Christmas card. This was not an easy decision, but Jim was hoping that a card might heal the breach between the two of them.

"At least I'm willing to make the first move," Jim told his wife Martha. "I'm tired of avoiding him" — which is pretty hard to do in a town this size, I might add.

Ernest, always the suspicious one, felt there was an ulterior motive in the card.

"Look at this," he said, handing Jim's card to his wife. "What do you think he's up to?"

"Well, the note says he'd like to apologize for the misunderstanding two years ago," Margaret responded.

"Well, why now?" Ernest wondered aloud. "You know what I think, I think he's trying to get on our good side in case he needs wood from the wood lot for this blizzard."

I guess Ernest had an interesting New Year's Day. Ernest turned in about 10 p.m. on New Year's Eve, figuring he'd need a good night's rest to face the rigors of no electricity, phone, water, and the like, the following day, due to the blizzard.

Of course, he wasn't surprised waking up to a cold, eerily quiet house. There was no power, but the phone was working. "Just a matter of time before the phone goes, too," he thought to himself as he lit the fire in the fireplace.

When Margaret got up an hour later she was greeted with an almost manic husband.

"I guess everybody will have to admit WOPE was right on this one," Ernest ventured.

By noon, when no one had called or stopped by for assistance, Margaret offered to call around town.

"Let's check on Carl and Coralie and the Heslers," she said.

"Go ahead," said Ernest with just a touch of gloat in his voice.

I suppose if Ernest hadn't been so downcast as he walked to the side of their house where the circuit breaker box was, he would have noticed the tracks in the snow and perhaps figured from their small size exactly who had shut off his power shortly after midnight. It was a modest problem, limited, as it was, to one home for about twelve hours.

"What are we going to do with all that firewood?" Margaret asked Ernest at dinner.

"Oh, we'll use it. You know it'll keep," Ernest said somewhat dejectedly.

"Did you send Jim a Christmas card like I asked you to?" she inquired.

"No, but I'm going over right now to see if he needs some wood," he answered.

What is it Carl says? "Every day is judgment day; use a lot of it."

No mail today, so I'll email you this. Our mail carrier Mr. Hurley (and the rest of town) is enjoying this new year without a blizzard. I trust you are, too.

Love to all,
Elizabeth

Worry/Trust
Therefore I tell you, do not worry about your life, what you will eat or what you will drink, or about your body, what you will wear. Is not life more than food, and the body more than clothing? (Matthew 6:25)

Dear Mike,

Well, church got out late on Sunday. I didn't get too much out of the last half of the sermon. It was a moving sermon. Most of us had moved on before the conclusion. Some of Reverend Answers' sermons make you feel dumb on one end and numb on the other.

Actually, I think most of us were numb from the cold weather. Winter has finally arrived. What is it Carl says? "It's so cold even the wind is howling about it." Wally, the weatherman at WOPE Radio, didn't realize how cold it was until he got the first-time touch of winter: his heating oil bill. Of course, that's understandable. Carl says Wally is someone with whom the weather seldom agrees.

But the rest of us could tell. I have my own way of telling when winter arrives. The windshield scraper that falls out of the glove box all summer is lost under the seat, and, once found, snaps in two when you go to use it. I have to admit this is as cold a winter as we've had in a while and a fair amount of snow has fallen so far, as well. It's been the major topic of conversation down at the Busy-Bee Café the last couple of weeks.

I don't know how many people at the Busy-Bee noticed that Meg, Sandy, Cheryl, and Blaine's wife, Carolyn, weren't there last Tuesday. I believe most people were too caught up in the noon television broadcast from Punxsutawney to notice.

These four have been getting together once or twice a month for about eight years. They began to have lunch together and to also do some needlepoint. Carl said, "It gave them something to think about while they were talking." They soon dropped that and tried their hands at bridge. Meg never could get the hang of that. She said she had a one-trick mind.

Carl says, "A good bridge player displays a triumph of mind over chatter." So bridge playing passed from the scene. For a while they would read one of the books from Oprah's Book Club, but eventually they came to the place where they knew they needed no pretense for getting together. Carl says, "They like each other in spite of their virtues."

So they meet every other Tuesday. Half the time at one of the four's home for lunch and half the time they go out to eat. Unless it's a special occasion, they'll stay in town and have lunch at the Busy-Bee on the out-to-eat days.

I suppose it was the egg salad sandwiches that got the other three thinking about Carolyn. Every time Carolyn hosts the luncheon the menu features egg salad sandwiches. You know, Mike, it's easy to see someone's actions but not easy to understand her motivation. Slowly, I think all three women arrived at the conclusion that Carolyn didn't have the money. This is especially true now that the Refrigerator Magnet Museum is in financial trouble.

Two weeks ago, as the luncheon was breaking up at the Busy-Bee, Meg took Carolyn aside and handed her a couple of twenties.

"I want you to use this for our next lunch. Let's go someplace wonderful," Meg said under her breath.

Carolyn was surprised with the gift, but even more surprised when a note came from Cheryl the next day with two twenties saying she wanted her to use it *all* for the next lunch. "Let's go someplace different," she wrote, closing the note.

I think you can guess what happened next. Yes, Sandy got Carolyn aside, pushed an envelope into her hand, saying, "I had a little something extra this month that I'd like you to use when we go to lunch next time. Let's make a day of it."

I think all three were surprised to get notes saying to be ready about ten on Tuesday as Carolyn would be stopping by to pick them up for lunch.

Tuesday was bitterly cold. The wind chill at 6 a.m. was twenty below. It had been a clear, cold night.

"Where are we going for lunch?" Meg asked, snow crunching under foot, as she got into the van with Carolyn, Sandy, and Cheryl.

"Over in Lansing, that's why we're leaving early," was all Carolyn would say. Each of the others tried to imagine where they might be going. Actually, each was feeling quite pleased with herself for helping Carolyn out.

I suppose if any of the three had been observant she might have noticed the picnic basket behind the backseat — but no one did. By the time Carolyn eased the van onto Michigan State's campus everyone's curiosity was fully aroused, perhaps relieved as they headed through campus. No one could voice the unthinkable: "Surely we're not eating in a college cafeteria."

At the south end of campus where the agricultural college test fields and dairy barns are, there is a small cluster of buildings that I don't think any of the van's passengers had noticed before.

Carolyn eased the van between two dairy barns and asked the others to get out and follow her.

"Hand me that picnic basket, will you?" she asked Sandy, who was seated closest to it.

"Picnic basket?" their minds simpered in unison.

More than one of the friends began to think she'd thrown her forty dollars away. Lost in their own thoughts as they were, they had failed to notice the one building that was semi-sheltered by a low knoll.

Even as they approached the hothouse, it hadn't dawned on them they could use it for a picnic spot.

Once inside the mood changed immediately from questioning to mirth as coats, hats, and gloves came off. It was like stepping into paradise after the cold of Tuesday. The air was warm, moist, and filled with the scents of tropical plants and the sounds of birds singing. Believe it or not, there are even a few finches and parakeets to control the insect population.

"This is heaven," Cheryl said, voicing the group's opinion as Carolyn set out the food for the picnic.

"How'd you find it?" "How'd you get the use of it?" "How long can we stay?" questions flew as the women strolled around looking at the plants.

"It's just a light picnic lunch," Carolyn said, as she placed the waxpaper-wrapped sandwiches on each enameled plate. "But the caretaker picked some figs yesterday that we can eat," she continued, "and I've brought a bottle of Zinfandel. You know, it's hard to find the right wine for egg salad."

Well, I'd better get this in the mail before Mr. Hurley, the mail carrier, gets here. I'm praying for you and that congregation.

Love to all,
Elizabeth

Good deeds/Spirits changed
They are to do good, to be rich in good works, generous, and ready to share.... (1 Timothy 6:18)

You have turned my mourning into dancing; you have taken off my sackcloth and clothed me with joy. (Psalm 30:11)

Dear Mike,

Well, church got out late on Sunday. I didn't get too much out of the last half of the sermon. If Reverend Answers was a storekeeper, he'd have a dry goods and notions store. Carl says the three keys to a great sermon are: be sincere, be brief, and be seated. We're hoping Reverend Answers can get at least two out of three. If the truth be known, I was admiring the flowers on the altar: a dozen red roses, very appropriate for the Sunday after Valentine's Day. I think I recall reading somewhere, "Flowers were the sweetest thing that God created and didn't put a soul in."

These roses were a Valentine's gift to Cynthia Weise, and she'd brought them to church. Carl says, "In the language of love, roses are fine, but tulips are better." But these roses have such a good story that they may actually be better than any flower. Each Valentine's Day these roses arrive for Cynthia with an enigmatic note from a secret admirer. This year's note said, "Old flames burn forever."

And each Valentine's Day, Darnell goes through the same routine. He goes through the same list of possible admirers, asking Cynthia if she thinks it could be this one or that. Year after year, he seems no closer to discovering who it might be. The flowers are delivered from different florists from Lansing and when Darnell has called to see who they're from, the florists just says they had been asked to maintain the strictest of confidentiality. So it goes each year.

While Darnell is stewing, Cynthia can't help but feel sort of enchanted by the whole business. She knows from experience how the rest of the day will go.

She'll make Darnell's favorite meal, which surprisingly is liver and onions. I believe that's his favorite because that was one dish that was at least consistent as he was growing up. To say his mother wasn't much of a cook is to be kind. They used to say about her, "What she doesn't know would fill a cookbook." Carl says, "The only thing worse than a wife who can cook and won't, is one who can't and will," and I guess that just about described Ruby. The one dish she never ruined was liver and onions (which some might contend was ruined beforehand, so what difference did it make); after all, how much worse can it get? Ruby's famous quote to the kids at mealtime as they were growing up was, "Hold your nose and swallow." So Darnell arrived at adulthood thinking liver and onions was a pretty fair meal and more importantly, knowing that sometimes you have to just "hold your nose and swallow."

So Darnell mopes around the house while Cynthia floats around the kitchen, both knowing full well how the rest of the evening will go. Over dinner she'll say, "Why don't I take the flowers to church for Sunday, then Reverend Answers can take them up to the hospital when he visits so and so on Monday," which doesn't go a long way in putting things right, but it helps.

And slowly, Darnell begins his routine, "Well, it's certainly understandable why you'd be getting flowers. You're as perfect as a person could be. You are still a beauty. I know I don't deserve a wife like you. You could have any number of the men around here. In fact, it's a wonder you only have one secret admirer."

To which Cynthia replies with a lilt in her voice and a twinkle in her eye, "Ah, that's the only one you know about." She sets the table with their wedding china and puts out the candlesticks with candles as he talks. I guess she could repeat his speech if need be. And every year the same — roses, candlelight, and liver.

Over dessert, with a certain flourish, Darnell produces an elaborately wrapped package. It is always a dress from Jacobson's in Lansing. Always striking. One thing you can say about Darnell, he has an eye for beauty. The tissue is turned back; the dress removed, held up for inspection, and suddenly tears are flowing. Then Cynthia's arms are around his neck and they kiss. They've done it so often they can do it with their eyes closed. What is it Carl says? "A kiss is something you can't give without taking and can't take without giving."

Cynthia runs to try on the dress. She knows that it cost more than she'd ever spend on herself. Like most of us, she shops the end-of-season sales and stores a little less pricey than Jacobson's.

Darnell tells her how beautiful she looks and it's true. She has on a dress she won't be able to wear out of the house for at least a month, maybe two. It's a spring dress. Of course, some of the winter dresses are on sale now, but when your wife has a secret admirer you don't shop the bargains.

I guess most of us know or at least suspect who that secret admirer is; it's no secret really. The flowers are ordered the same day the dress is purchased.

But we all admire the roses on the altar — a mute testimony to old flames burning forever.

Well, I'd better get this in the mail before Mr. Hurley, the mail carrier, gets here. We're praying for you and that congregation.

Love to all,
Elizabeth

Appreciation/Love/Valentine's Day
Better is a dinner of vegetables where love is than a fatted ox and hatred with it. (Proverbs 15:17)

Let him kiss me with the kisses of his mouth! For your love is better than wine.... (Song of Solomon 1:2)

Dear Mike,

Well, church got out late on Sunday. I didn't get too much out of the last half of the sermon. Reverend Answers has been trying to include a joke or two in his messages lately. Our congregation has a keen sense of humor. The more he humors us, the better we like it. In reality, though, most of us have been out of humor the past month or so.

The weather hasn't helped, either. In fact, it's part of the problem. We had such a mixed winter that we all expected an early spring. I half expected to have most of my garden in by now. That has not proved to be the case, however. The Saturday before Easter we had snow, not a lot, but enough to force the Sunday school Easter egg hunt into the church basement, which would have been fine, had it stayed in the basement. But one or two of the youth who helped hide eggs put more than a few upstairs in the sanctuary. Of course, none of the kids looked up there for them. So Easter Sunday when a few were spotted upstairs, we just assumed they'd been left behind by one or more of the kids.

The Sunday after Easter a few more eggs were discovered. This time it wasn't our eyes that found them, but our noses. Carl said, "They that smell the least, smell the best," and "These eggs are composed of what's decomposed." We all had a good laugh and hoped that was the end of it.

The following Sunday it was obvious that still not all the eggs had been found. Carl was quick to point out that "whoever had hidden the eggs was first rank."

As bad as that was, there was a bigger stink brewing (so to speak). You may recall Annie Lockwood. She's started dating a man named Buddy Harris from over at Chapin, and it looks like a real relationship might develop for them. He's been coming to church with her for the last few months and during that time he's caused quite a stir at church.

He wears the same jacket each week; no, not a sports jacket or a suit jacket, but a tan and black satin jacket that was a promotional give-away. Embroidered, or as some say emblazoned, across the back are the words MGD Light with a couple of checkered flags. The front sports a similar figure, only smaller.

You know the Lockwoods sit down toward the front on the pulpit side. Most of the church gets a good look at the back of Harris' jacket every time we stand to sing.

Well, some are saying it's not appropriate dress for church, and others are saying it doesn't matter. I will say it has created a fair amount of tension. On the one hand, no one wants to ruin Annie's last chance, perhaps, at a stable relationship. But others are saying they can't worship staring at a beer sign. And if they wanted to stare at a beer advertisement they'd just as soon do it at Gallagher's.

Carl, to his credit, has been counseling everyone to not get too stirred up about it. He's been saying, "If we want harmony in the church, everybody has to quit harping." Frankly, I don't think we need harmony. I think we need hush money. At least I'd like to get a few to hush up about it. You know how Ernest Porter is once he gets an idea in his head.

Two weeks ago, Ernest decided to take the matter to Reverend Answers. Ernest wasn't sure that Reverend Answers even knew what MGD Light was. In fact, I don't think many of us were sure if he knew. After all, it's hard to gauge exactly how worldly a pastor is.

"You've got to get Annie's boyfriend to stop wearing that jacket," Ernest buttonholed Reverend Answers after church.

"What on earth for?" inquired Reverend Answers.

"Because none of us can worship when he's wearing it," Ernest answered.

"I can't believe it's the jacket," Reverend Answers replied, wondering where this conversation was going.

"Let me ask you straight out," Ernest continued, "Do you know what 'light' is?"

Reverend Answers paused just for a moment, realizing this was not a theological question *per se*, and then answered, "Yes, something that travels inconceivably fast until it encounters the human mind."

"Not that light," Ernest fired back, perhaps proving the correctness of Reverend Answers' definition. "Have you seen that jacket that Buddy is wearing? What do you think the letters MGD Light stand for?" Ernest pressed his case.

"My Gracious Deliverer — Light of the World," responded Reverend Answers, hoping against hope. "Why?"

"You're wrong, it's a beer, and that jacket has no business in church. I want you to talk to him about his dress," Ernest finished up, not knowing if Reverend Answers really didn't know about beer or not.

"If it's that distracting," Reverend Answers offered in a conciliatory manner, "why don't you sit down front?"

"Because when I go to church I want to sit in my own pew," was Ernest's final comment on the subject. And that's what we've been doing all month, sitting in our own pew.

Last week was unusually warm, so by Sunday the church had been aired out and the last of the spoils of Easter had been found and carefully removed. I can't say when Annie has looked better. She had on a beautiful floral print dress, and Buddy had left his jacket at home. In its place, a polo shirt with his name embroidered on the breast pocket — "Bud."

I'd better get this in the mail before Mr. Hurley, the mail carrier, gets here. We're praying for you and your church.

Love to all,
Elizabeth

Phariseeism/Judging others

Do not judge, so that you may not be judged. For with the judgment you make you will be judged, and the measure you give will be the measure you get. Why do you see the speck in your neighbor's eye, but do not notice the log in your own eye? (Matthew 7:1-3)

When the Pharisees saw this, they said to his disciples, "Why does your teacher eat with tax collectors and sinners?" (Matthew 9:11)

Dear Mike,

Well, church got out late on Sunday. I didn't get too much out of the last half of the sermon. Reverend Answers used lots of quotations. Carl said, "He spoke volumes."

If truth be told, there was an undercurrent of tension at church Sunday, as there has been in town for the past month.

I suppose we've all known for some time that Glen Morris was going to sell Secluded Acres. It has never been profitable as a golf course, more a labor of love than anything else. Years ago, it was pasture land. In fact at some point, one of the owners planted Osage orange trees and boxwood as hedges. I assume the high hedges are what gives the course its name, although I don't recall just now what it was called when Glen bought the place some twenty years ago.

Carl said at the time of the change, "They turned the cows out of the pasture and let the bull in." And around this time each year, Carl would say, "Spring is here — time for the farmers and golfers to start plowing."

Well, there won't be any jokes about golf this year, as the course has new owners and a new direction. I don't think anyone in town took notice in February when word spread that the Hyde Park Association had bought the 380 acres. I guess most of us just assumed they'd take over the course.

I mean who would have thought that Hyde Park was a nudist colony? What is it Carl says? "They're the only cult that gives you the bare facts."

Well, some of the facts that have come out are: 1) Secluded Acres was perfect because of its high hedges, rolling hills, pond, parking, small clubhouse, no zoning restrictions, and general remoteness from any population center; 2) the Hyde Park Association only uses the facility from Memorial Day to Labor Day; and 3) the barest fact of all, they go around naked.

I must admit it has been lively down at the Busy-Bee Café, as there's been not a little discussion on people's rights, freedom of speech, NIMBY (Not In My Backyard), and such.

Carl has had a field day with this change. He said Secluded Acres was an obvious choice for a Nudist Association. "They're all excellent golfers," he opined. "They go a whole round in nothing."

And he's warning anyone who'll listen, "They'll have a million followers by summer — mosquitoes," which if true, might reduce the numbers out on my side of town and be a direct benefit.

Carl said, "Going to a nudist camp is like flying on an airplane. It's the first take-off that's the scariest."

But joking aside, there is a lot of tension and difference of opinion on this turn of events. Last Saturday afternoon, a town hall meeting was scheduled at the high school for people to voice opinions, and one of those with the strongest opinion surprisingly was George Wilson. For whatever reason, George is dead set against the nudist camp coming in. He'd gone so far as to print up petitions, looked into changing zoning laws, told everyone who'd listen his position, and seemingly expected everyone to fall in line with his thinking. In fact, he was the one who pushed for the town hall meeting.

George had planned on arriving well in advance of the meeting to greet people and "work the crowd." So he was glad he'd started early when he found his car wouldn't start. He went next door to John and Cheryl's to see who could give him a jump. Matt was the only one home. John and Cheryl had conveniently arranged to be out of town and not be embroiled in George's controversy.

"Matt, I don't know if your battery's too weak to turn over this Cadillac's engine or it's something else, but we're not going to get it started with jumper cables," George said as he removed the jumper cables. "Can you run me into town?"

"Grandpa, I've got to get ready for tonight's prom," Matt replied.

"Well, it's getting late and I need to get to the school. Can I borrow your truck?"

Matt knew he could hardly say, "No," but he sure hated to let George drive off in it after he'd just had it "professionally cleaned" for the prom.

"Okay," Matt said reluctantly as George climbed into the driver's seat.

George had barely eased out of the driveway before he began sniffing the air. "What's that smell?" he wondered, and maybe more importantly, "Where's it coming from?" In another minute or two he'd placed the odor — "Bubble gum," but he couldn't find its source. How could he, he hadn't been at the carwash when they gave it a spray of Bubble Gum Scent air freshener that Matt had picked for the prom.

George wondered if there was a piece stuck to him or the seat, and he jiggled himself around trying to feel for a wad of gum.

"It's got to be on the floor mat or my shoe," he said aloud, looking at his feet and bending forward to check with his hand.

It was then that he took his eyes off the road just long enough to drive onto the shoulder. Jerking the light pickup's steering wheel only caused it to skid slowly on the wet earth into the ditch and thus ending a promising political career. The mud in the ditch made it impossible for the truck to unstick itself. So George waited for some help.

In the meantime people in the gym at school discussed, without too much enthusiasm, the new neighbors.

Frankly, Mike, it's hard to generate much debate in a room that's decorated like a cruise ship sailing in the South Seas, although I had an eerie feeling it was supposed to resemble the *Titanic*. The town council reported that legally there was little they could do to stop the purchase and use of the golf course as a nudist camp.

George finally got Matt's truck out of the ditch, but by then the meeting had broken up. And no real decisions were made.

"Listen, Matt, I'm sorry about your truck; I threw quite a bit of mud up on it trying to rock it out of the ditch," George relayed to Matt. Matt only heard a couple words, "mud, ditch, stuck."

The interior was just about as bad, at least the driver's side floor mats were!

"By the way, you've got a piece of bubble gum stuck in one of the floor mats," George said.

Both were thinking with a note of sarcasm, "This is a perfect way for the most important day of the year to unfold."

I'd better get this in the mail before Mr. Hurley, the mail carrier, gets here. We're praying for you and that congregation.

Love to all,
Elizabeth

Acceptance/Strangers/Lifestyles
Welcome one another, therefore, just as Christ has welcomed you, for the glory of God. (Romans 15:7)

Do not neglect to show hospitality to strangers, for by doing that some have entertained angels without knowing it. (Hebrews 13:2)

... the Son of Man has come eating and drinking, and you say, "Look, a glutton and a drunkard, a friend of tax collectors and sinners!" (Luke 7:34)

Dear Mike,

Well, church got out late on Sunday. I didn't get too much out of the last half of the sermon. Sometimes it seems that Reverend Answers is not only preaching for posterity, he's waiting for it to arrive. Sunday he got done before he finished.

If truth be told, I was anxious to get home as I'd baked a rhubarb pie in the morning and was in a hurry to have a piece before it got too cool.

In fact, the whole service had a tartness one might associate with rhubarb. There was some tension in the air at church around the whole issue of the Hyde Park Association's Memorial Day weekend opening of Secluded Acres (as a nudist camp). I don't know that there was much opposition at church other than George Wilson, but there was still a general uneasiness about the topic. I mean, after all, we're talking about nudity. George had gotten the nudist camp to agree to provide a security officer on the premises throughout the summer, with the understanding that they'd press trespassing charges against anyone caught "lurking around."

"They'll be prosecuted to the full extent of the law," George would tell anyone who'd listen.

Carl was having a field day down at the Busy-Bee Café telling everyone, "The nudist camp is the place where every morning brings the dawn of a nude day," and "Don't blame a person for being a nudist, they're born that way," and so on.

Actually, Carl has been preoccupied the last few weeks trying to get Honduras into better shape, so we've all been spared some *pun*ishment. About a month ago Carl and Coralie took Honduras in to see Blair Richardson, the vet.

"That dog's twenty pounds overweight," Blair told Carl and Coralie. "You've got to start exercising him."

"What do you suggest?" Carl asked.

"Jogging with him, or at least walking, and get him some lower calorie food," Blair continued.

It didn't take Carl too long to realize that he wouldn't be able to keep up the jogging pace that even an overweight Honduras liked. One thing led to another and the final solution was Carl riding his bike and Honduras trotting along beside him on a pretty good-sized leash. I guess they do five or six miles a day.

I've occasionally seen them go past my place, moving at a pretty fair clip. Evidently, the exercise is paying off. Honduras is losing weight, and, if truth be told, I believe Carl is, too.

But Tuesday, Carl came face to face with a design flaw in the exercise plan. They were out on Reed Road on the far side of Secluded Acres when a rabbit dashed across the road in front of them. Honduras was after it in a flash, jerking Carl and his bike into the ditch. They were tail-over-teacups in a twinkling. Carl was quite shaken, the bike's front wheel bent beyond use, and Honduras off in the underbrush beyond the ditch sniffing for the rabbit.

Carl's face was scratched up like someone had taken sandpaper to it, his glasses bent, and his ankle twisted. He finally composed himself enough to get Honduras and start for home. It was too early for much traffic, and he'd purposely chosen a road with few or no cars as a safety precaution. As he moved along, the pain in his left ankle seemed to get worse with each step.

He knew he had at least two miles to hobble if he circled around Secluded Acres. Carl figured the shortest route home — or at best to a more heavily traveled road — was right through Secluded Acres. He assumed that being early in the morning few, if any, people would be awake, and he could slip by unnoticed and unnoticing.

He was almost correct. As he neared the Osage orange hedge on this side of Secluded Acres, he heard the hum of a golf cart behind him. His first thought was "Here's help," until he saw the word "Security" emblazoned across the windscreen. "Come on, Honduras," he said, crawling through the hedge at just the last minute.

But Honduras had thoughts of his own on the matter.

"Come back here," the security guard called out to Carl. "I've got your dog. You'll be charged with trespassing," he continued.

Carl limped on home.

"What happened to you?" Coralie asked, "And where's Honduras?" she continued in the same breath.

"He joined a cult!" Carl answered. "I've got to ice my ankle; it's killing me."

"How'd you get so cut up? And just look at your shirt; it's cut to ribbons." As if Carl hadn't noticed.

About an hour later, the security man from the Secluded Acres showed up with Honduras and asked for Carl. "Honduras, you get in here. Have you been causing trouble?" Coralie volunteered in a cheery voice as she welcomed the dog home.

"Listen, sir, I'm sorry if he's put you out. He does stray from time to time, and I sure do appreciate your bringing him home; that's what the tag is for," Coralie fired off in rapid succession.

"I'm actually here to talk to your husband," the security man began. "We have a matter of unlawful trespassing to discuss."

"Why, that's impossible," Coralie started. "You see, it was just one year ago today that my husband was killed in a freak accident out at Secluded Acres. He was hit in the head with a golf ball and dragged behind his golf cart. Our dog here has been bereaved ever since and occasionally goes out to try to find him. And now you are trying to tell me they've been seen together."

"I'm sorry, ma'am," the security guard began, "but that's the worst excuse I've ever heard."

"Well, my husband is the writer in the family," she said, smiling.

"Thanks, honey," Carl said a few minutes after the security man had left. "But if they were going to arrest anyone it should have been Honduras. You know dogs aren't allowed. The rules clearly say, 'No short pants permitted.'"

Well, I'd better get this in the mail before Mr. Hurley, the mail carrier, gets here. We're praying for you and that church.

Love to all,
Elizabeth

Shortcuts

When Pharaoh let the people go, God did not lead them by way of the land of the Philistines, although that was near; ... So God led the people by the roundabout way of the wilderness toward the Red Sea. (Exodus 13:17-18)

You're A Winner
July 1

Dear Mike,

Well, church got out late on Sunday. I didn't get too much out of the last half of the sermon. Reverend Answers gets a little nervous this time of year as the giving drops off. So he drags out his "Sermon on the Amount." Really I don't know why he preaches, "Give until it hurts." He knows we all have low thresholds of pain. Last Sunday, Reverend Answers' sermon was what Carl calls a bicycle wheel: longer spoke — greater tire.

Speaking of bicycles, have you noticed these men out on bicycles? I swear I've yet to see a look of enjoyment on any of their faces. Carl says they don't smile to keep the bugs out of their mouths. When you see a kid on a bike, they have a look of downright joy. But I swear these men look like they're riding away from an accident as fast as they can. Now a kid on a bike looks like she's going somewhere, which may very well be the case. If you ask me, they've wrung the joy out of bicycling by putting on those tight pants and sitting on that tiny seat.

You should have seen the look on Mike Wilson's face a week ago Thursday as he pedaled home from work. He's been hired to clean up at the Refrigerator Magnet Museum three days a week. What is it Carl says? "Employers believe hire should be lower." To be sure, Mike is at the lower end of the pay scale. I suppose he was lucky to find any kind of work during the summer, because he is only fifteen years old. You know the Refrigerator Magnet Museum business is a lot heavier in the summer. During most of the year they're only open on weekends, and Blaine and Carolyn pretty much handle it. But this time of year people come from all over. Why, two or three times a week tour buses stop on their way to Frankenmuth or Chesaning.

Well, Thursday was busy and by 8 p.m. when Mike started home, he'd earned his minimum wage per hour. Blaine asked him to detail the parking lot one more time and then put the chain across the entrance.

118

It was as Mike was locking the chain that he noticed the yellow spot just at the edge of the blacktop. If he'd picked it up differently he might have missed the writing in the bottle cap. But right there were the words, "YOU ARE A WINNER."

And that was the look that he had on his face as he pedaled home, "I Won!" Of course, he wasn't sure what. He just started up the hill on Hibbard Road when his brother Matt slowed in the truck.

"Grab hold of the door handle and I'll tow you to the top," Matt said.

"I'm a winner!" Mike shouted into the car over the radio that was playing just a hair shy of eardrum-damage level.

"Have it your way," said Matt as he pulled away thinking Mike was declining the help.

Mike spent the night with the family trying to decide what exactly he might have won. It was decided that the logical thing to do was ride over to Bradley's Market on Friday and find out what company had bright yellow caps on their bottles and then contact them. John and Cheryl had cautioned that perhaps the contest had expired. But Mike was convinced he'd won something.

Walt Bradley was pretty sure he'd never seen a cap like it. "Try one of the big stores over in Lansing. Maybe they can help," he offered.

That was how Mike and Matt spent Saturday. Matt, by now, was saying he rightfully should share in the prize: a finder's fee of sorts. But Mike was keeping promises to a minimum. "We'll have to see what the prize is first." They had no luck on Saturday, either. But Mike wasn't about to give up, even if it meant calling every 800 number in the book.

Sunday, during the "Sermon on the Amount" an idea started building in Mike's head. After all, he was a winner! Mike was busy the next couple of days and Wednesday he showed his idea to Blaine.

I guess Mike had made up about 100 bottle caps with a message on the inside and a magnet on the back. He'd spent hours on the computer making up the small circles, printing them out on clear laser labels.

119

Most said, "YOU ARE A WINNER." A few said, "GRAND PRIZE WINNER" or "TRY AGAIN." Two said, "BETTER LUCK NEXT TIME." Mike's idea was for the museum to sell them in the gift shop. Blaine knows a good idea when he sees one. He told Mike he had a winning idea on his hands. "You make them, we'll sell them. I'll give you your own refrigerator door in the gift shop," Blaine said.

The first 100 were sold out and Mike cleared $100. I bought one for myself that said, "YOU ARE A WHINER." It could have been a typo, I suppose, but if the shoe fits....

Oh, yeah, Matt solved the mystery of the cap last week. Of course, by then I don't know if winning a case of brake fluid was very important. Yes, it was a cap off a bottle of brake fluid. When Matt bought some for his truck Thursday, he noticed the display: bright yellow bottles with twist off caps and signs saying, "You're a winner with Lucky Brakes products."

"Mike, how can I break this news to you?" Matt began when he got home. "I know what contest your cap is from and the prize isn't going to do you much good," he continued. "Actually this is going to break you up."

Well I'd better get this in the mail before Mr. Hurley, the mail carrier, gets here. We're praying for you and that congregation.

> Love to all,
> Elizabeth

Persistence/Character/Hope
And not only that, but we also boast in our sufferings, knowing that suffering produces endurance and endurance produces character, and character produces hope, and hope does not disappoint us, because God's love has been poured into our hearts through the Holy Spirit that has been given to us. (Romans 5:3-5)

But I will hope continually, and will praise you yet more and more. (Psalm 71:14)

Honduras In Trouble
August 4

Dear Mike,

Well, church got out late on Sunday. I didn't get too much out of the last half of the sermon. Don't get me wrong, it was a first-grade sermon. Unfortunately, most of us are beyond first grade. Some of Reverend Answers' sermons are like eating an artichoke: so much roughage for so little substance.

Frankly, with this heat it's hard to concentrate on much of anything. I guess we're in the midst of dog days. I know for a fact that Carl and Coralie are. Let me back up a little bit.

I think you're well aware that Carl's dog, Honduras, likes to go off on a lark every once in a while. Carl has had to haul him home from any number of places, but in March he was surprised to get a call from Henry Fairchild at Pets 'n' Stuff.

"You better come get your dog," Henry began, "and we'll need to talk."

"What's he doing at a pet store?" Carl asked.

"He's not at the store," Henry answered. "He's at our house."

"He's certainly social," Carl allowed, trying to get a reading on Henry's mood.

"Yes, that's what we'll be needing to talk about when you get here," Henry said as he hung up the phone.

"Carl, we've got us a little problem here," Henry said, leading Carl around the back of the house to the kennels. Carl had assumed that Henry had put Honduras into one as a holding place until Carl got there to take him home.

"What's Honduras doing in there?" Carl asked, looking at the kennel holding a short-haired pointer and Honduras.

"That's the socializing I wanted to talk to you about," Henry began. "Can you guess what a litter of pups with Rachel's bloodlines is worth? Thousands!" he said, answering his own question. "Rachel has won every competition there is. Her pups are in great demand," Henry said drawing out "great," sort of like Tony the Tiger.

"Are you telling me Honduras is going to be a father?" Carl asked, emotion draining from his voice.

"Well, only time will tell, but look at him and you give me your opinion."

Carl had to admit there was a certain smugness about Honduras that he hadn't seen before.

"Carl, I'm a reasonable man," Henry began to set out his conditions. "We can't have this happen again. Rachel only has one or two litters a year. It's a shame to lose one to Honduras. We have to make sure he doesn't come calling again."

"You want me to have him destroyed?" Carl asked, with dread creeping into his voice.

"Destroyed?" Henry couldn't believe his ears. "No, just get Dr. Richardson to fix him."

"Oh, okay," said Carl, with a sigh of relief.

"There's one other thing," Henry continued. "You'll need to take the puppies once they're weaned."

"No problem," Carl agreed quickly, thankful that he wasn't going to have to make some financial restitution to Henry for Honduras' night of romance.

It took Carl over a week to make the appointment for Honduras at Dr. Richardson's, and then only after Coralie's nagging.

"You'd think you're the one having the operation," Coralie said to Carl.

"Well, I'm just waiting for the right moment to break the news to Honduras," Carl replied, knowing she was about half right.

"Here," she said, handing Carl the cordless phone and reading off the vet's phone number. "It's not like we're depriving the dog gene pool of anything special."

"Henry told me to expect you and Honduras," Blair said.

Carl thought better than suggesting that Blair and Henry (with his taxidermy skill) go into business together, although he wanted to tell someone he'd come up with a great slogan for the new venture, "Either way, your pet goes home with you."

"You really should have had this done years ago," Blair was saying to Carl, who wasn't paying too much attention as he was distracted, looking at the big chart of dog breeds in the examining room.

"You can't imagine that much variety, from big to little, cute to ugly, long hair to short hair, you name it," Carl commented.

122

"That's what comes from living in too close proximity with humans," Blair responded rather philosophically. "Your mixed breeds are often healthier and better dispositioned dogs anyway."

"What are you saying, Blair, that maybe we shouldn't go ahead with the operation?" Carl asked, grasping at straws.

"What, and deprive me of my fee?" Blair joked, "No, this is the right thing to do. Come back tomorrow afternoon for him."

On the drive home Carl was feeling relaxed enough to imagine crossing a breed or two to come up with his own.

"How about a Lhasa Apso and Shitzu cross? That would be a Lhasa Shitzu," he mused.

Not much time for musing for Carl these days; eight of the cutest puppies you ever saw arrived last Tuesday.

Carl's plan is to find good homes for them in the next couple of weeks. He's advertising them on his website, *e-mote*. "Fancy dogs for dog fanciers, champion bloodlines."

"Why name them?" he asks Coralie. "Look how friendly they are. They'll all go through life thinking their name is 'Downboy' anyway."

"That one looks just like Honduras," Coralie says, pointing to the male with the dark brown muzzle. "Let's call him Champ." The real reason Carl has resisted naming them is knowing that would just create a bond.

Well, I'd better get this in the mail before Mr. Hurley, the mail carrier, gets here. We're praying for you and that church.

Love to all,
Elizabeth

Actions have consequences
... *for you reap whatever you sow.* (Galatians 6:7b)

Named
The Lord called me before I was born, while I was in my mother's womb he named me. (Isaiah 49:1b)

Dear Mike,

Well, church got out late on Sunday. I didn't get too much out of the last half of the sermon. Reverend Answers' sermon was on "the milk of human kindness"; unfortunately, it wasn't condensed. If the truth be told, I think most of us were in awe after the unveiling and our thoughts were on the freshly renovated mosaic floating above our pastor's head.

I'm sure you remember the mosaic of Mary in the basement hallway. Late last spring, Coralie was watching the PBS *Antiques Roadshow*. What is it Carl says? "Antiques often aren't as old as they're cracked up to be." At any rate, she saw a mosaic tabletop that put her in mind of the mosaic downstairs. The table, I might add, was appraised at $20,000.

Coralie began to do some research on our "Madonna Mosaic," as she had taken to calling it, which you'll agree is better than Carl's "The Maybe Virgin." The main question, of course, was whether it was done by the DeMorgan brothers, as was the table on television. But a couple other questions were also raised.

I don't know if anyone had actually gotten a good look at the mosaic, mounted as it was in a hall. You always had to look down the hall at it, rather than square on because the hall isn't even six feet wide. On top of that, over the years several tiles had been lost, a film of dirt had covered tiles and grout, and the trustees at some point had put a Plexiglas pane over it to stop the slow trickle of lost tiles to the hands of our church school kids.

When Coralie got the appraiser from Detroit, the first thing he said was, "Why'd you put something this valuable in the basement?" And, as they say, "Therein hangs the tale."

"How'd a Methodist church get a Virgin Mary mosaic anyway?" he asked Coralie. "I mean usually you'd expect this mosaic with this subject matter in a Catholic or Orthodox church."

Let's go back to the beginning. Evidently, there were three years in the 1920s when the DeMorgans were in New York working on tiles and mosaics for the Louis Comfort Tiffany and Company, often making or designing tiles and mosaics for churches to go along with Tiffany's stained-glass windows. One of our pastors from that era, a certain Reverend Branston, was quite taken with the mosaics.

"It's the most religious art form," he told the quarterly conference where he raised the idea of a mosaic for our church. "Think of it as a metaphor for the church of Christ: universal and triumphant. It is the historic medium for expression of permanent truths." I'll bet church really got out late in his day.

Whether he was very popular or a better speaker than the quarterly conference records suggest, he must have been a good fundraiser, because it was finally agreed he'd contact the DeMorgans about a piece. The suggested subject matter would be Jesus as the Good Shepherd and, as much as possible, Jesus should look like John Wesley.

The DeMorgans sent two large mosaics from their studio in New York City in the summer of 1929. The first stop was at the Trappist Monastery in upstate New York. The abbot was aghast at what he saw when the workman uncrated the mosaic.

The madonna was deemed way too beautiful — sensual might be a better term. She might well have been the poster girl for collagen lip enhancement therapy had she lived in this era. "Pretty as a picture — nice frame, too," as we've all heard Carl comment as he has walked past the mosaic. The abbot politely told the workman the piece wasn't going up on the refectory wall. It would be impossible to keep the brothers' thoughts on things spiritual with a madonna that looked like that, he reasoned.

"There must have been some mix up. What else do you have on the truck?" So the deliveryman showed the Good Shepherd. "You see, they mislabeled the mosaics in New York," the abbot told the driver as he and the monks were unloading the artwork.

There was the same uproar here. Everyone suspected the pastor was pleased with the "mix-up," as he dragged his feet in trying to clear it up.

Anyone who saw it, swore the madonna with her great shock of red hair, aforementioned "frame," and full pouting lips bore an uncanny resemblance to Willa Branston, "the lovely pastor's wife."

125

Of course, from this later date it's hard to tell, as we don't have any photos of her. Just as it is hard to tell exactly what "lovely" is modifying.

By the time the dust had settled, as it were, the Depression had hit and the DeMorgans had returned to England, leaving behind a small, but significant body of work, and at least two less than fully satisfied customers.

The madonna was in limbo during the next ten months as the church debated where to install her. It was finally decided to relegate her to the basement hall where she has suffered silently all these years.

. Well, she suffers in silence no more. The restoration process took most of the summer. Once the restoration was complete, she was moved to the chancel. Last Sunday was the unveiling. We'd all seen glimpses, but Mike, it was awe-inspiring. There were audible gasps throughout the congregation. Not a one us of doubted the $500,000 appraisal, nor the reason the abbott had made the switch.

The piece is absolutely incandescent. It glows — it burns — there is fire! The light from the altar candles swims and splashes around in the gold and iridescent tiles. The gilded tiles, against the cerulean blue in particular, capture your eye. Carl says he thought the church should be taking gilt out of the world, not adding it.

The efforts of Coralie and the Restore-the-Virgin Committee could not have gone better. And I'm pleased to report that many of the members at St. Mary's contributed to the fund, as did many of the town's people.

It's comforting, too, to think that somewhere in upstate New York at least one monk must be silently wondering why Jesus looks like a white haired, seventy-year-old English cleric as he shoulders a sheep back to the fold.

Well, I'd better get this in the mail before Mr. Hurley, the mail carrier, gets here. We're praying for you and that congregation.

Love to all,
Elizabeth

Beauty
One thing I asked of the Lord, that will I seek after: to live in the house of the Lord all the days of my life, to behold the beauty of the Lord, and to inquire in his temple. (Psalm 27:4)

Finally, beloved, whatever is true, whatever is honorable, whatever is just, whatever is pure, whatever is pleasing, whatever is commendable, if there is any excellence and if there is anything worthy of praise, think about these things. (Philippians 4:8)

Nature of the church/Many parts, one body/Mosaic
As it is, there are many members, yet one body. (1 Corinthians 12:20)

Dear Mike,

Well, church got out late on Sunday. I didn't get too much out of the last half of the sermon. Reverend Answers' message was kind of like the weather, dry and windy. In fact, it's been so dry I think most of the church was praying for rain Sunday, although I'll admit none of us brought umbrellas to church.

I'd say *almost* everyone was praying for rain. I'm sure Helen and Henry Fairchild were hoping for good weather, as they'd signed up for a fall-color tour of northern Michigan, with three days and two nights on Mackinac Island. Carl said the travel folder Henry was showing around at the Busy-Bee was a "trip tease." And Carl says, "The people who go on those bus trips are mo-tourists."

Helen had trusted Henry to make the arrangements with a travel agent in Lansing, but Henry kept putting off doing it. Helen wasn't going to nag. She doesn't enjoy travel, and I suppose she was hoping the tours might all be filled before Henry got around to it. She almost got her wish.

Helen spends most of her vacation wondering whether she turned off the stove, left a faucet running, unplugged the coffee pot, locked the doors, and numerous other things. When Henry says, "Don't worry about it," she says, "That's easy for you to say; all you do is get in the car and honk the horn."

Last Monday, Henry was still trying to decide if he should mention that he had been a little slow in making reservations for the coach tour.

"You wouldn't mind if this is a seniors' tour, would you?" Henry asked.

"Why no, not at all. I suppose this time of year most of the people on tours are senior citizens," Helen opined.

"We might have single rooms at the Grand Hotel on Mackinac. That wouldn't ruin it for you, would it?" he continued, wondering if this might be the time to drop the bomb.

"No, I suppose not. By the way, did I leave a night-light on in the downstairs bathroom?"

"Let the record show she changed the subject," Henry thought.

Henry decided he'd see how long he could go without confessing that the only tour that wasn't completely full when he finally called last Wednesday was the Single Senior Citizens' Fall Fantasy. He'd made two reservations, one for him and one for Helen, using her maiden name.

They had a nice lunch at the orchard in St. John's and Helen went to the restroom while Henry got back on the bus. Helen was surprised when she got back on the bus that a strange woman was sitting next to Henry and engaging in quite an animated conversation.

Helen stood in the aisle waiting for the woman to move. Henry, always the quick thinker, got up and insisted Helen take his seat. He moved forward to an empty seat behind the driver. "Maybe this isn't going to work out after all," he mumbled to himself.

"Now there's a real gentleman," said the woman. "I'd like to catch a man like that."

Helen looked around the coach. Slowly the reality of the tour dawned on her. "I'd like to catch one like that, too!" she said hoping the sarcasm wasn't showing.

"Have you been on these tours before?" Helen asked.

"No, but a cousin of mine has gone on a couple and actually met a man she's been dating on a Frankenmuth day trip."

Mackinac Island was beautiful. The trees were at full color. The timing was perfect, right between the time the bare limbs of people move to the bare limbs of trees.

Henry was having trouble enjoying it, though. As he sat in the white wicker chair on the Grand Hotel's porch Tuesday evening, he had a delicious, two-pound problem. He was holding in his hand a box of Mackinac fudge, a big box, recently delivered by the concierge, with a note, saying, "With affectionate thoughts. Meet me at 7 o'clock on the west porch. XOXOXO."

This was uncharted territory for Henry. He was pretty sure it was from the woman who had flirted with him in the horse-drawn carriage that morning. After all, he'd shared some fudge with her.

I suppose I'll just have to tell the woman I'm married, he thought. But what room is she in? What's her name? What's she look like?

"No, I better start with Helen," he said to no one as he rose from the chair.

Of course, he couldn't find her and it was already 6:30.

At 7:00 the woman from the carriage rounded the corner of the porch. Before he said anything, the woman from the bus seat incident came out through the dining room doors. Then another he didn't think he'd even met before. And finally the trump card, Helen.

"Anybody care for a piece of fudge?" Henry asked sheepishly. Try as they might, they couldn't keep straight faces.

It dawned on him, Helen had set him up.

When they got back Thursday, Henry said, "All expense tour" pretty much says it all. Carl said, "When you return from a vacation, it's hard to settle down, but harder still to settle up." I think that pretty much describes Henry's situation.

Well, I'd better get this in the mail before Mr. Hurley, the mail carrier, gets here. We're praying for you and that congregation.

Love to all,
Elizabeth

Folly
Fools die for lack of sense. (Proverbs 10:21b)

Forgiveness
Forgive and you will be forgiven. (Luke 6:37b)

... and be kind to one another, tenderhearted, forgiving one another, as God in Christ has forgiven you. (Ephesians 4:32)

Dear Mike,

Well, church got out late on Sunday. I didn't get too much out of the last half of the sermon. In fact I almost didn't go to church; it had rained hard just after daybreak right up until I got to church, although it is dry inside (which is the other reason I didn't get too much out of the sermon). What is it Carl says? "Oh, Reverend Answers works hard at preaching, but it is a thinkless task." Don't get me wrong, I could listen to Reverend Answers forever, and sometimes I feel I have.

But if truth be told, my mind was distracted by the recent election happenings. Carl says, "Politics is the most promising of careers." As far as I know this is the first time the presidential candidates have stumped the states both before and after the election.

Our weather has reflected the indecision of the election perfectly. It can't seem to decide if it really wants to be winter. We'll have a day or two of glorious Indian summer and then a gray freeze, then rain, then some snow. The leaves are all pretty well off the trees, repaying the earth for the green that the summer lent. Some days it smells so good with the scents of the season and the next day there is a sour smell that spoils everything. I wish I could say the sourness is limited to the seasonal shifts.

Frankly, it seems the weather is just a reflection of the mood here in town: argumentative, with some sourness thrown in. I'm glad our presidential elections only come every four years. I assume the founders of the United States realized, as I now do, that most communities couldn't survive one more often than that.

There seems to be an observable political split between the people who live in town and those of us out in the township, although family loyalties do play an important part. Take the Lockwoods as an example. You know she was a Porter before she married Rob. His family has always been town people. They've had the hardware store forever. Now the Porters have farmed out this way for three generations. And I don't think I have to remind you of the kind of person Ernest Porter was during elections.

Actually, the Lockwoods have a good marriage. As proof, I offer that it has withstood the rigors of seven presidential elections. Joan takes one candidate and Rob the other. And they're both pretty vocal in their support of the respective party and candidate.

I remember four years ago things got so bad that Joan blurted out, "Rob, I'm actually looking forward to canceling your vote." One thing led to another, and before long they decided they would just both stay home and not vote. It did seem small to Joan to think she'd be happy canceling her husband's vote.

About noon on election day, Rob thought he'd go over to the school just to see if the turnout was heavy or light. Well, once there he thought, he'd just go ahead and vote. Can you imagine Joan's surprise when she recognized his shoes in the booth? Can you imagine Rob's surprise when he pulled back the curtain and looked his wife square in the face? It was three days before he had the nerve to inquire as to the purpose of her visit to the polling place.

As I said, that was four years ago and pretty much limited to one family. The Busy-Bee Café has been all but empty the last couple of weeks. Nobody wants to get caught in a booth with the town's most vocal political experts. Carl has tried to ease the tension with humor. He'll crack, "You know a politician shakes your hand before the election and your confidence afterward."

Carl has probably added to the stress.

Anyway, Wednesday morning at 10:30, a time of day when the Busy-Bee Café is usually filled with people who've stopped off for a coffee after picking up the mail, or getting something at the hardware store, or just in town to catch up on the latest news, it was empty except for Darlene, the waitress. Dwight and Arlene had gone to Lansing to buy for the restaurant. And Rex, the cook, who lives out back in the Airstream trailer, was taking a mid-morning break inasmuch as there were no customers.

Darlene knew immediately who the stranger was before he sat down at the counter. Oh, he'd lost some hair, it was gray at the temples, and he'd put on some weight, but there was no doubt about it when he said, "Hello, Darlin'."

132

It was Elvis. Darlene was sure. She's such a big fan that she's insisted as a condition of her continued employment that Dwight and Arlene keep "Are You Lonesome Tonight?" on the juke box.

He had three jelly doughnuts.

Darlene kept hoping someone, anyone, would come in to witness Elvis being there.

He paid with a ten-dollar bill and told her to keep the change and said, "The service was special, darlin', know what I mean?"

He drove off in a big yellow and tan Lincoln.

Well, all day Thursday and Friday, the town was all a-buzz. About half the town saying, "Yes, it probably was Elvis," the other half saying, "No, it was Jimmy Hoffa or someone who just looked a lot like Elvis." Carl kept suggesting we have a recount to decide.

It's nice to have people arguing about something else and not divided along political party lines.

Oh, occasionally someone will say, "Did you say he was driving a Lincoln?" Makes me think Lincoln was the last good Republican president. But things don't go much farther than that.

Me? Oh, I don't know. Carl says whoever it was, it was a man of note. I suppose you can guess what's playing on the jukebox at the Busy-Bee now: "All Shook Up" and "Are You Lonesome Tonight?" both *apropos*.

Well, I'd better get this in the mail before Mr. Hurley, the mail carrier, who by the way I've heard humming "Don't Be Cruel," gets here. We're praying for you and that congregation.

Love to all,
Elizabeth

Relationships
See to it that no one fails to obtain the grace of God; that no root of bitterness springs up and causes trouble, and through it many become defiled. (Hebrews 12:15)

Dear Mike,

Well, church got out late on Sunday. I didn't get too much out of the last half of the sermon. I'd like to say it was a good sermon: I'd like to. I looked high and low for the point Reverend Answers was making. But evidently, I didn't look low enough.

I suppose I was still a little done in from Christmas. What is it Carl says? "It's the season when people keep their radios on for hours on end, playing 'Silent Night.'" Actually it was listening to Christmas music that gave Carl his idea for Coralie's Christmas gift. He had the radio on in his old pickup as he was coming home from Lansing, where he's taken what he refers to as seasonal employment in one of the department stores.

I don't think I'll be speaking out of school, when I say Christmas is hard on Carl. After he and Coralie closed the weekly newspaper five years ago Carl hasn't really had a steady job. Oh, he substitutes at the junior high school and high school, and he's still trying to make a go of his email newsletter, *e-mote*. But if truth be told, he and Coralie are always short on cash and the holidays only exacerbate it. Carl tries to maintain his sense of humor about it. He'll say things like, "It's not just Santa who's in the red this year," or "The ideal gift is money, the trouble is you can't change it." Last year he told everyone, "Coralie's gift to me of a billfold was the height of irony."

At any rate, as he was driving home from the mall where he's been working, he heard a version of the "Twelve Days Of Christmas," and by the time they got to the lords-a-leaping verse, Carl knew what he wanted to get Coralie.

The next morning he was up at Pets 'n' Stuff when Henry opened the doors. I'd say they've pretty well made up since their Honduras' trouble last summer. I put most of that on Helen and Coralie, who in the midst of heated words were able to provide some perspective. I think some conversations move along like cars on the highway, smooth flowing, and then they notice an accident, and slowing to look are drawn into an accident themselves. Fortunately, the wives kept them headed away from the accident.

"What can I do for you?" Henry asked.

"Well, I'm looking for a gift for Coralie," Carl answered.

"You've come to the right place if you want to give her something mounted. How about one of these bucks?" Henry asked pointing to a small forest of antlers.

"I was actually thinking along the lines of something a little more lively," Carl replied. "Do you have turtledoves?"

"What about a canary, a parrot, or a parakeet?"

"Oh, yes, I want a pair," Carl said interrupting Henry and trying to make a joke. "What would we do with one keet?"

Henry didn't slow down to look at the accident but kept moving forward, "Why don't you try Mr. Sorda, he's got pigeons, doves, and a smattering of smaller birds. And he often gives them to good homes."

Carl was trying to picture what turtledoves might look like as he drove out to the Sordas. Carl found Abe out by the lofts where he was tending a couple of nests of newly hatched homing pigeons.

"How you doing, Abe?" Carl said by way of greeting.

"What brings you around?" Abe answered, with just a hint of Flemish in his pronunciation.

"Well, sir, I'm looking for a pair of birds that would be a good Christmas gift for my wife," Carl explained.

"House birds or outside birds?"

"I guess inside, I don't know for sure. Do you have a recommendation?" Carl answered.

They spent most of the morning going from loft to loft, Abe talking and gesticulating as they went. Carl could see his natural affinity with the birds, as several times he mistook Abe's hands for the flutter of wings.

"I've got two main strains of homing pigeon out here," Abe explained as they neared the loft with the white birds.

"These are raised to be released at weddings, funerals, and special occasions, and over there are the poor man's thoroughbreds," Abe continued with pride filling his voice as he nudged his head toward the larger loft where the racers were housed.

"Do you ever mix the two strains?" Carl asked.

"Well, I do, although most breeders don't — too much trouble," he continued.

"What do you mean?" Carl asked.

"Well, take these two squealers, for example. Now that they've molted, I can see they aren't going to be pure white. What most breeders do is just destroy the mottled chicks. But I'll use some in cross breeding with the racers."

"Doesn't that dilute the gene pool of the racers?" Carl asked getting into the conversation.

"Maybe yes, maybe no," Abe answered. "You see it isn't just athleticism that makes a good racing pigeon. It's heart or spirit — or an intangible. It's hard to tell right away because it doesn't show up on the wing or breast. It's in the heart."

"I suppose you could say the same about people," Carl suggested, or even Christmas gifts he thought to himself.

"Poor man's thoroughbreds?" Carl thought to himself. "With their ability to navigate home, I'm thinking poor man's global positioning service. And if you did get really lost and hungry, well...."

Carl steered the conversation back on the subject of gifts. "You know why I stopped, would you have anything that might be a good Christmas gift for my wife?"

Carl was thrilled as he headed back to town with the two Gouldian finches in the small bamboo cage on the seat beside him. "Coralie's going to love these," he thought to himself as he listened intently to their songs.

And he was right. Coralie was overjoyed with the gift. "Oh, Carl, they'll brighten the house on gray days, their music will cheer us each day, and most importantly, they'll provide hours of entertainment for my Christmas gift to you," she said, handing Carl the big sock that seemed to have a life of its own. It did, what with the bob-tailed kitten inside.

Well, I'd better get this in the mail before Mr. Hurley, the mail carrier, gets here. We're praying for you and that church.

Love to all,
Elizabeth

Inner person/Gifts

But the Lord said to Samuel, "Do not look on his appearance or on the height of his stature, because I have rejected him; for the Lord does not see as mortals see; they look on the outward appearance, but the Lord looks on the heart." (1 Samuel 16:7)

If you then, who are evil, know how to give good gifts to your children, how much more will your Father in heaven give good things to those who ask him! (Matthew 7:11)

Section 4:
Two Years Ago

Sprinklers
January 7

Dear Mike,

Well, church got out late on Sunday. I didn't get too much out of the last half of the sermon. I'm afraid I have trouble concentrating on Reverend Answers' sermon. Carl says a wandering mind is a triumph of "mind over prattle." Last year at this time, Reverend Answers announced his New Year's resolution was to make shorter, more interesting sermons — the good die young.

I think Carl is right when he says we'd all like a "low podium diet" this year.

I doubt if anyone had much success paying attention to Sunday's message. Christmas is still too much with us. This was not an easy December for Carl and Coralie. They went through most of Christmas without much good will or good humor worrying about their finances.

Cheryl and John Wilson weren't doing much better this year. The boys, Matt, who is a senior, and Mike, who is a junior, are becoming fairly demanding. Both of them had long want lists, which meant when they got most of the things they'd asked for they weren't really surprised, much less very appreciative. Cheryl had mulled this over for a few days. Several gifts had been expensive. Both John's parents and hers had purchased expensive gifts for both boys. Not gifts to be shared, mind you. And here it was five days after Christmas and neither boy had written thank-you notes.

"Why don't you write those thank-yous? You know Ann Landers doesn't want to get a letter from me signed 'mother of two ingrates,' " she prodded.

"We already thanked them in person," Matt replied.

"Well, that's not the same," Cheryl responded, tension rising in her voice as she tried to be heard above the iPods plugged into their ears.

Being heard above the music was a problem Reverend Answers had Christmas Eve at the candlelight service. This year I was in charge of the "Hanging of the Greens." The church never looked better, if I do say so. We put garlands of Douglas fir around the windows and across the altar rail, all tied with white ribbons — simple, yet lush.

I'd hoped for the warm glow of candlelight, so we used the two large candelabras and put individual ones on every other pew and in the windows. Mike, it was beauty itself. And I'm not the only one who thought so. As if that weren't enough, the weather cooperated so on Christmas Eve the church was packed. I know a few people had to stand.

You can probably recall how we conclude the service with the congregation lighting candles and singing "Silent Night." Mike, it was perfect: the church full of happy people singing of their faith, bathed in the warm glow of candlelight. Radiant!

I guess we were on the third verse, singing, "... shepherds quake at the sight, glories stream from heaven afar," when the quaking began, complete with the streaming from heaven.

All the heat generated by the candles tripped off the church's new sprinkler system. Although I don't believe for a minute there was any danger of fire, the heat sensors located in the ceiling (near the pulpit, I might add) felt a raging inferno had already broken out. Mike, you'd be amazed at how much water that system can deliver in just a couple of minutes and how cold it can be.

We never finished the singing. The shouts and screams ruined the mood, which was already dampened. Hairdos fell, fur coats that only see the light of day on Christmas Eve looked like wet cats, and people ran for the door as if their lives actually depended upon it. All the while Reverend Answers was shouting, "Stay calm! Stay calm!" in one of the most agitated voices I've ever heard.

I won't go into further details. Fortunately, the Lockwoods, who installed the system, knew where the shut-off valve was and got the water stopped before everything was soaked.

Carl said to me later, "Wouldn't you know it, a major story and the paper already folded. Maybe I'll do one more issue." Coralie just rolled her eyes.

I spent much of Tuesday cleaning up the mess. Frankly, I was feeling a little bit sorry for myself. I'd worked hard to decorate the church and received not one single note of thanks for my efforts. I mean, if you ask me, the Lockwoods ought to be apologizing for ruining Christmas, and they're going around town saying how the sprinkler system saved Christmas and untold lives.

I suppose it could have been worse. Carl has been saying, "Christmas Eve candles almost make light of everything" would be a good opening line for a lead story on the event. I'm trying to make light of it, but it isn't easy.

Well, I'd better get this in the mail before Mr. Hurley, the mail carrier, gets here. We're praying for you and that congregation.

Love to all,
Elizabeth

Giving thanks/Christmas
Surely the righteous shall give thanks to your name.... (Psalm 140:13a)

Then Jesus asked, "Were not ten made clean? But the other nine, where are they?" (Luke 17:17)

Dear Mike,

Well, church got out late on Sunday. I didn't get too much out of the last half of the sermon. Carl said that it was the type of sermon that appeals to the church pillars. And I always associate pillars with sleep! Actually, so many people have been missing church I'm beginning to think our denomination is becoming Seventh Day *Absentists.*

Not that there aren't good reasons people aren't in worship. The weather is still terribly cold and the roads are icy in places, which makes it hard for some to get out. Others have been under the weather with the flu and colds. What is it Carl says? "A cold is the only thing that can stay in some people's heads more than a day." A few people are out of town. The Fairchilds are in New York City. I believe I've written about how high they are on one of the pointers. Turns out they are right. Rachel received an invitation to be part of the second oldest sporting event in the United States: The Westminster Kennel Club's annual show. She is a beautiful dog, white and lemon, a muzzle that is picture-perfect in profile and well proportioned.

In some ways, this trip is a dream come true for Helen. After she and Henry sold the Pets 'n' Stuff concept to the Detroit investors, she's felt like she could use another challenge. It goes without saying the corporate owners are pleased to have "one of theirs" in the spotlight at Madison Square Garden for this 125th show, not only for publicity but for the obvious financial benefits. They've gone so far as hiring a handler who has shown Rachel for the last year.

Henry decided if they were going to New York they'd go in style, so just after Christmas he bought a Lincoln Town Car. Admittedly, it's a bit showy for these parts, but to his defense it is two years old. Before the trip he had it fitted with a screen so Rachel could lounge in the backseat and not ride cooped up in the travel kennel.

They tell me that dogs are judged on temperament and conformation. Well, if temperament has any part of it, I'm predicting

Rachel will be a champion. Carl says, "She may be a pointer, but she's so polite she'll only nudge and nod her head."

Carl ought to know, as his dog, Honduras, has had more than a passing interest in Rachel. Fact is, Carl feels they're family. And he and Honduras are raising one pup, Champ, to prove it.

Well, early last Friday, just before daybreak, Henry, Helen, and Rachel eased out onto the highway in the black Lincoln Town Car. Henry's plan was to drive to Pennsylvania the first day and on to Manhattan the next. As they started out Saturday, Helen couldn't help but notice that Rachel wasn't her usual self. And by the time they got to New Jersey she was sure something was wrong. Henry, in the meantime, was cheerfully cruising along.

"Pull over at the next rest stop," Helen told Henry. "I want to give Rachel some exercise and a liver snap or two." (I might add I sent along the tin of liver snaps as my contribution to this quest.)

"Maybe the ride is too long for her," Helen guessed, "but she's definitely not herself. She's off her feed. She's lost her enthusiasm, I just don't know what to think," she continued in a worried tone.

"Let me ride in the backseat with her the rest of the way," Helen continued climbing into the back.

Mike, geographically New York City is less than 600 miles from Maybe, but conceptually it is light years away. For example, it would never occur to someone out here that anyone would actually use Lincoln Town Cars as taxis, but in New York City they make up half the fleet. Here we think a taxi should be yellow, not black, and maybe a Crown Victoria or an Impala now that the Checker Company is out of business.

"Honey, look how friendly these people are. I didn't think Carl knew what he was talking about when he said New Yorkers were standoffish and brassy," Henry said, hoping to lighten the mood in the backseat as he headed the car down Central Park West and wondering just how Carl had come by his information. "I mean people are literally stepping off the sidewalk and waving at us," he continued. "Fact is, you'd think they wanted us to stop and visit."

145

"Look, look there," he said, pointing and waving to the couple who seemed mystified at Henry's friendliness and had themselves quit waving.

"I guess the mayor's campaign to make NYC friendlier is paying off," Henry opined.

When they slowed for a traffic light at Columbus Circle a woman in a mink coat stepped off the curb and waved. Henry, ever-friendly, smiled and waved back, a sign the woman took to mean Henry was for hire.

To say Helen was surprised when someone opened the door to get in back with her is something of an understatement. To say that the view Rachel had of all that fur must have touched some primeval fear of bears would be dead on.

Hackles up, teeth bared, Rachel growled, snarled, barked, and was just about to lunge at the beast, when the woman slammed the door and beat a hasty retreat.

"This isn't the same dog we left home with," Helen said, anxiety creeping into her voice.

Henry, on the other hand, was enjoying the friendliness of the city.

"What happened back there?"

"You go through life missing everything, don't you?" Helen exploded. "Didn't you see the woman in the fur coat?"

"Yes, yes, I did. Do you think she killed it herself?" Henry mumbled under his breath.

All three occupants were out of sorts when Henry turned the car into the hotel's underground parking garage.

"When we get checked in I'm calling Blair Richardson. This dog is sick," Helen told Henry.

Carl had used almost the same words to Coralie as he gazed down at Honduras in the kitchen that evening.

Well, I'd better get this in the mail before Mr. Hurley, the mail carrier, gets here. We're praying for you and your congregation.

Love to all,
Elizabeth

Companionship/Grief

Two are better than one, because they have a good reward for their toil. For if they fall, one will lift up the other; but woe to one who is alone and falls and does not have another to help. Again, if two lie together, they keep warm; but how can one keep warm alone? (Ecclesiastes 4:9-11)

Dear Mike,

Well, church got out late on Sunday. I didn't get too much out of the last half of the sermon. It was what Carl calls a "ginger ale sermon" — "It goes flat before the finish." Of course, my mind was distracted as this was the first Sunday everyone was back from New York City. Our attention was on our two heroes.

I think you'll recall how upset Helen was that Rachel, their prize-winning German short-hair, was feeling blue by the time she, Rachel, and Henry got settled in the hotel near Madison Square Garden. Evidently, it is a favorite of those showing dogs at the Westminster Kennel Club Show. But Rachel didn't even seem to notice the other dogs. They checked in and the lobby was, as Carl would later say, "a virtual welcome waggin', " but Rachel didn't even notice.

Carl had been concerned about Honduras all that same day, and at about 4:30 he called Blair Richardson to see if he should bring Honduras in.

That evening, when Helen called from New York describing similar symptoms, Blair knew what the problem was.

"Separation anxiety," he declared to Helen.

"Oh, come on, how can that be? We're here with her," Helen rejoined.

"You're not the one she's missing," he said. "It's Honduras."

Carl was the next to receive a call from New York.

"How would you and Coralie like to come to NYC?" Henry asked in his most endearing voice.

"No, we can't leave. Honduras is under the weather," Carl replied.

"Bring him with you." This was going easier than Henry had hoped.

"We'll pay for everything," a phrase no one would have expected to hear from Henry.

By the time Helen had talked to Coralie, everybody had a pretty good idea of exactly why they were needed in New York.

"Get packed!" Carl barked at Honduras. "You're an army dog now. You're getting a new post."

Honduras was in no mood for humor and wouldn't be until Thursday when they got to the hotel on 34th Street.

Even the most casual observers could have seen the light go on in the dogs. They were half beside themselves. Carl would say the hotel exchanged hard-earned dollars for small quarters. But he was pleased with the arrangements.

"Well, that was the tonic she needed," Helen said to Carl and Coralie as they watched the dogs frolic in the room.

Tuesday was the preliminary judging. As Helen and Henry left for Madison Square Garden, they could tell Rachel was getting anxious again.

"We'll never get Honduras into the show," Helen said to Henry, her mood falling about like Rachel's. "And I don't think she'll show well without him around."

"Let's go back to the hotel and see what we can come up with," Henry advised.

"No problem," Carl answered upon hearing the request. "Get me a pass. I know what to do."

"What kind of dog is that?" the security man asked Carl as he scrutinized Honduras.

"Bull terrier," Carl replied.

"He seems awfully big to be a terrier." The security man continued, "I didn't know they were using mixed breeds as 'seeing-eye' dogs."

"Something new," Carl replied.

"Nothing personal, buddy," the security man asked, "but why would someone with a vision impairment such as yours come to a dog show?"

Quick as a wink, Carl replied, "Oh, I'm not here for me. This dog likes to schmooze." As if on cue, Honduras began wagging his tail in earnest.

It couldn't have gone better for Rachel that day. In fact, by the end of Tuesday it was obvious, even to the one blind man who was haplessly wandering around into areas marked "Restricted: Handlers Only," that Rachel was a lock on best of breed.

Wednesday allowed her to claim best of group honors as well. And, who knows, she might have beaten that Bichon Frise for best of show had not Carl decided to step out with Honduras for a hot dog.

As he was about to eat the hot dog, Carl asked Honduras, "Well, buddy, what do you think of this for a headline — 'Man Bites Dog'?"

But no one complained that day. That was saved for Thursday.

Henry was explaining to Carl and Coralie how the puppies from Rachel's next litter had just increased in value by a factor of ten.

"You're surely not thinking of breeding her?" Carl stated, shock obvious in his voice.

"Why not?" Henry asked.

"Why not!" Carl's voice rising. "I'll tell you why not. Think of Honduras' feelings."

"Are you out of your mind, they're dogs. What feelings?"

"We drive all the way here from Michigan because she's feeling blue and you ask me 'What feelings?' " Carl fired back.

"Rachel's a gold mine," Henry volunteered.

"How much money do you need?" Carl asked in a pained tone.

"I'll give you first pick from the litter," Henry countered.

"You just don't get it, do you? I have a pup from the last litter, don't I?" Carl came back.

And that's the way it was left, as far as I know. Now I think you can see the real reason I didn't get too much out of the last half of the sermon.

Well, I'd better get this in the mail before Mr. Hurley, the mail carrier, gets here. We're praying for you and your congregation.

Love to all,
Elizabeth

Money/Relationships/Loyalty
But those who want to be rich fall into temptation and are trapped by many senseless and harmful desires that plunge people into ruin and destruction. (1 Timothy 6:9a)

Wedding Pigeons
April 1

Dear Mike,

Well, church got out late on Sunday. I didn't get too much out of the last half of the sermon. I'd say we've given Reverend Answers the best ears of our life. Carl said, "Reverend Answers sure knows how to spin a yawn." But if truth be told, our eyes were all on the recently returned honeymooners sitting down toward the front on the pulpit side of the nave. What is it Carl says? "When they return from the honeymoon the cooing stops, but the billing goes on forever."

The new bride looked radiant and the new groom a lot more relaxed than usual. It was a wonderful wedding, albeit unusual in this sense, it wasn't on a Saturday. But you know how the Lockwoods are, and Annie is no different. They all travel to the beat of a different drum. In fact, that is probably the reason she waited until she was 37 to marry. It was Buddy Harris' second marriage, which Carl said was a triumph of hope over experience.

But it was that theme of hope that led Annie to choose the vernal equinox as the day of their wedding. This is the time of year when there is more light each day, in our part of the world, than darkness. So it could easily be construed that this would make a beginning of more love in their lives. To the less quixotic, perhaps the thought occurred that at least Buddy would be able to remember his anniversary. And, who knows, it might have been something of a jest to all those who were displeased that Buddy always wore an MGD Light jacket to church. As I said, you never know about the Lockwoods, Annie included.

Be that as it may, the wedding was quite lovely. The church had never looked better. And this was the first wedding since the mosaic was installed in the chancel, which lent beauty to all the bridal party. The candles just gleamed against the gold and blues of the tiles. Reverend Answers had a nice message on the key to a happy marriage: "The husband gives and the wife forgives." Carl said, "They'd taken each other for better or worse — better for Annie, worse for Buddy." But who knows?

Annie had the service end just before sunset so there would be a warm glow on everyone as they left the church. She'd also arranged for Abe Sorda to release about a dozen of his white homing pigeons as the couple exited the building. Neither he nor the pigeons are strangers to the church. As you may recall, Reverend Answers had the birds released on Easter a few years back, something I believe he saw Robert Schuller do on television once.

But actually, this has become a nice sideline for Abe, releasing white "doves" at weddings. He has a magnetic sign on the door of his pickup that reads: "Say it with Flyers." He'll put a crate down with a drape to keep the birds quiet and at the prearranged time release them, or shoo them out for their flight home, in this case about twenty miles.

As Annie found out in making the arrangements, homing pigeons mate for life — a good omen she thought. The birds usually have a brood of two chicks, or squealers, as the bird fanciers call them, and have an uncanny ability to get back home. During the racing season, the females who have chicks at home often perform better than males as they "fly to brood," although both parents share in sitting on eggs and feeding the chicks.

"Here, hold one," Abe told Annie as he gave her the tour of his birds and coops.

"It feels heavier than I expected," Annie told him, not knowing exactly what she'd actually expected a pigeon to weigh.

"There're just three differences between a homing pigeon and the pigeons you find in the park," Abe continued as if he was about to reveal one of the great secrets of life. "They are more muscular, they wear a band, and they can find their way home."

Had Carl heard that, I've no doubt he would have said, "That's what every bride wants in her groom."

There may be a fourth difference, as we were to find out as the happy couple exited the church simultaneously with the birds' release at the end of the walk. The sidewalk was lined with well-wishers, all of whom cheered and welcomed them with a shower of birdseed. These birds, living as they do, aren't the least bit bothered by humans, so when they saw all that birdseed they just swooped back down for a snack before heading home. I'm sure that would have been fine had not one of the birds decided that the easiest pickings were on Annie's veil, now pulled back from her face and over the train. Somehow in a flash of wings and arms, the poor thing was all tangled up, the bird, I mean. And it took a while for Abe to catch it and get it free, all the while the veil attached on one end to Annie and the other to the pigeon's foot flapping about as if it had a life of its own.

Fortunately, things had calmed down considerably by the time the bridal party reached the VFW hall where the reception was held. Carl said, "We could pardon Annie's father if he shed a few cheers," and he did. It was a fun reception. One of Buddy's friends had even made a special handcrafted beer complete with labels he'd printed at Kinko's that said: "A New Groom Sweeps Clean."

Carl was quick to point out that the pigeons fly to brood, but that Buddy's friend brews to fly. Happily, the exertion of the day and night weren't too exhaustive for bird or man and all arrived home in good spirits.

Well, I'd better get this in the mail before Mr. Hurley, the mail carrier, gets here. We're all praying for you and your church.

Love to all,
Elizabeth

Wedding
Then the Lord God said, "It is not good that the man should be alone; I will make him a helper as his partner." (Genesis 2:18)

Let marriage be held in honor by all, and let the marriage bed be kept undefiled. (Hebrews 13:4)

Dear Mike,

Well, church got out late on Sunday. I didn't get too much out of the last half of the sermon. Reverend Answers is a man of great faith — faith in our patience. The sermon was what Carl calls a "coffee sermon" — "vacuum packed." In my opinion, coffee should have been served before it. I suppose there is a symmetry here — when Reverend Answers prays he closes his eyes; when he preaches he closes ours. But if the truth be told, my mind was drifting lazily like the clouds outside.

Those great, bulbous, cotton-puff clouds are but an additional sign that spring is here. You know, it's hard to say just when spring begins. Is it with the return of the robins? Or is it the redwing blackbirds? Is it in the first daffodil, first forsythia, or first lilac? Is it the first lamb or the first tadpoles? It's hard to say it's officially here at Easter, as Easter won't stay put.

Spring is sort of like that. One year it arrives fully dressed in March and the next you're halfway through April before you've even got half the garden in.

Carl is perhaps the best barometer of when spring arrives. I think you'll recall how Carl prides himself on having the first cook-out of the summer. And to make sure it's the first, he has been forced to move it into late April or early May.

Last Saturday was this year's date. I'm beginning to believe this global warming thing is for real as his barbecue arrives earlier each year. And, frankly, if you've ever seen Carl cook, you'd put a fair amount of the blame on him. You see, Carl doesn't hold back on the charcoal lighter fluid. I doubt if the pillar of fire and cloud of smoke the Lord used to lead the Hebrew children had anything on Carl's.

Needless to say, he goes through a Weber grill a year. A couple of years ago, Coralie had the idea of getting a gas grill in the hopes it would improve Carl's cooking and the environment. It was to no avail, as Carl refused to use it.

"You don't get the same flavor without the charcoal, Coralie," Carl told her.

"That's the point," Coralie replied. "Some people are more than a little tired of the taste of lighter fluid."

But Carl wasn't listening. Now don't misunderstand, Carl would be the first to admit that he hasn't been very successful as a cook. "Heaven sends good meat, the devil sends the cook," as Carl himself might say.

Bertha Wilson always said she didn't know what was worse, a man who could cook and wouldn't, or a man who couldn't cook and would. Frankly, I think Carl has answered that.

To compensate, we all bring along an "appetizer."

If Carl were more in tune with what was going on, he might quip, "Appetizers are what we eat until our appetites are gone," which is, after all, the point. Some years it's just hold your nose and swallow.

I think all of us have developed a slightly different strategy over the years on how to be diplomatic, eating just a bite or two and yet somehow giving the semblance that we're eating with relish and enjoying it.

My strategy has involved bringing in outside help. There was only one year that I couldn't get Carl and Coralie's dog, Honduras, to help out. Three years ago, the cookout fell on the Saturday before Mother's Day. As you know, Carl and Coralie have no children, but Carl always gets Coralie a gift from Honduras, and that year was no exception. Carl had purchased a Whitman Sampler for Coralie and had hid it in the garage.

Evidently, when he was getting out the grill from the garage, Honduras had gotten in and sniffed out the chocolate. Whether it upset his stomach or just filled him up is hard to say, but I know I couldn't get him to even nibble the hamburger I was surreptitiously passing him under the table.

This past Christmas, Coralie gave Carl the perfect addition or remedy to at least one of his cooking problems: an electric charcoal starter. Of course, none of us had much hope that the cooking would be any different this year, although I was hopeful there wasn't any chocolate lying around after Easter. So we all showed up fairly full from the heavy lunches we'd had at home.

Carl and Coralie had borrowed chairs and tables from the church and had them nicely arranged in the side yard. It was nice to be warmly greeted by my compatriot, Honduras, and his son, "Champ," named, I might add, in deference to his mother's lineage. They both looked hungry! I was elated.

Carl was at the barbecue in a white chef's hat and an apron emblazoned with "Kiss the Cook." At first I thought I'd arrived early as there was no aforementioned "pillar of fire, or cloud of smoke," just heat shimmering off the grill.

An hour later, nine of us sat down to the meal. I think I can speak for all of us when I say we weren't stuffed on appetizers, but pleasantly full. Shock of shocks, the hamburgers were delicious. These may have been among the best hamburgers ever, and we were too full to enjoy them. Cervantes is at least half right when he observes, "Hunger is the best sauce." Carl was justifiably proud, as he could tell he'd finally gotten it right.

Mike, you know I'm the type of cook who can forgive anything but a poor appetite, so I gave it my best, regretting that I couldn't enjoy it, not to mention not one, but two dogs under the table pawing impatiently for me to hand out the contraband. Like father, like son. At one point Honduras looked up at me as if to say, "You gonna finish that?"

If you'd told me that I'd ever ask for a "doggie bag" after Carl's cookout I'd have said "I'd already done that, only without the bag" but that is just what I did. I had to take along the half of hamburger I hadn't eaten.

"That's the best compliment I ever had," Carl told me as he handed the bag to me. "And to think you had seconds," he continued.

(Well, I did have to keep my dogs in on the scam just in case this year was a fluke.)

Well, I'd better get this in the mail before Mr. Hurley, the mail carrier, gets here. We're praying for you and your congregation.

Love to all,
Elizabeth

Beatitudes/Hunger for God/Bread of Life

Blessed are those who hunger and thirst for righteousness, for they shall be filled. (Matthew 5:6)

Jesus said to them, "I am the bread of life. Whoever comes to me will never be hungry, and whoever believes in me will never be thirsty." (John 6:35)

Cold Cream
June 1

Dear Mike,

Well, church got out late on Sunday. I didn't get too much out of the last half of the sermon. Reverend Answers says he needs a four-week vacation this summer. I say we need it more. Now Reverend Answers' sermons do have good points — at least they prick the conscience.

Actually, there's been something of a crisis of conscience going on at the Wilsons' house the last couple of weeks. I'm sure you'll be surprised when I tell you that their younger son, Mike, has been using a performance-enhancing drug over the past three years during the baseball season.

You know how important the high school baseball program is in this community. I suppose that alone adds pressure to the team. And Mike, of course, wanted to do at least as well as his older brother, Matt, who was part of two championship teams a few years ago. And I suppose, indirectly, his parents, John and Cheryl, put on pressure, just wanting Mike to have the positive experience of playing on a team and contributing to its winning efforts.

Three years ago this month, Mike made an unusual discovery. He'd been out most of the day and gotten too much sun. When he got home he searched the cabinet in his parents' bathroom for something to cool off the burning sensation. It was pure serendipity, but understandable. I mean who wouldn't use a product called "Cold Cream" on a sunburn?

I doubt if he got much cooling from it, but about fifteen minutes after applying it, he did begin to sweat, and sweat profusely from all the places he'd put the cream, virtual rivulets running down his face.

That following spring when Mike was trying out for the high school baseball team, Coach Olson told most of the players that they just didn't seem to be giving an all-out effort.

"Why, some of you boys have been out on that field for thirty minutes and haven't even broken a sweat," Coach Olson barked at them. The fact that it was March and probably no more than fifty degrees on the field didn't change Coach Olson's expectation.

The light bulb went on in Mike's head, and, sure enough, the next day just before heading out of the locker room to the field, he smeared a dollop of cold cream on his forehead, and for extra measure a swipe along the headband of his baseball cap.

And within fifteen minutes he was the coach's delight and the envy of about fifteen other boys.

"Wilson, I liked what I saw out there today," Coach Olson said as the boys headed off the field. "You're an inspiration to us all." And that's how it started.

At the awards banquet at the end of the season Mike was recognized as the most improved player and got the nod for the "Charley Hustle" trophy. Coach Olson, a man who most of his waking hours wears clothes referred to as "sweats," enthused, "We've never had a player work this hard. In all my years of coaching I've never seen so much sweat," pride filling his voice.

Of course, last year was just a repeat of that. Same awards, same speech from the coach, same pride from the family. If truth be told, Mike was uncomfortable with the adulation and awards, going so far as suggesting the coach consider someone else on the team who "might be more deserving." Coach Olson, in recognizing Mike's "Charley Hustle" award said, "This boy is so modest he even suggested naming someone else this year. Now that's what I call team spirit!" he bragged on Mike.

The sweat on Mike's brow that night was all natural. Embarrassment will do that.

This year might have been a repeat of the last two but for a cruel twist of fate. Ponds introduced a "new, improved" cold cream this spring. When Mike lathered up his forehead and cap for the first practice, nothing happened. "Maybe I need to use a little more to get the same effect," he thought. (A typical response from a user.)

It slowly dawned on him what the "new, improved" meant. He used the consumer 800 number on the box to confirm his suspicions. You can imagine his difficulty in asking the consumer affairs representative about the cold cream. As you know, teenage boys aren't Ponds' typical consumers.

"My mother asked me to call to find out about the improvements in your cold cream," Mike began.

"Yes, our chemists are always looking to improve our products," the representative answered.

"She's sort of grown attached to the old one."

"Well, the previous product did cause about one person in 10,000 to perspire," the representative explained.

"You don't say?" said Mike.

"Well, what if my mom wanted to get that original recipe?" Mike inquired. "Any chance it'll be like Classic Coke? You know, brought back by popular demand?"

"It's doubtful. After all, there's no call for a product that makes people perspire," the rep concluded.

Coach Olson really bore down on Mike during the beginning of the season.

"Where's the famous Wilson hustle?" the coach would ask after each practice. "You're not even breaking a healthy glow out there, much less a sweat. What gives?"

And every Saturday, Mike searched the smaller drug and grocery stores in hopes that they hadn't restocked, still carrying a few of the old formula.

Mike finally had to tell Coach Olson the truth.

I'm sure he was disappointed in Mike. "I don't think you need to give back the awards, but at the end of the season you'll have to tell your teammates, and if that doesn't make you sweat, then nothing will," Olson allowed. "It'll be just like a baseball game. The goal is to get home safely," he continued, grinning.

Mike was assigned one job to do as penance. You know how Coach Olson has hung all those placards with quotes around the locker room? "Winners Never Quit and Quitters Never Win," and the like. Well, Mike had to repaint the one above the baseball trophy case. It now reads: "Three Ingredients for Success: Aspiration, Inspiration, and Perspiration."

Each year Carl says about our team when they go to the state playoffs: "The cream of the team is either in the pitcher — or in the batter." Next year someone might just add, "or occasionally on a face."

Well, I'd better get this in the mail before Mr. Hurley, the mail carrier, gets here. We're still praying for you and your congregation.

Love to all,
Elizabeth

Accountability
For God will bring every deed into judgment, including every secret thing, whether good or evil. (Ecclesiastes 12:14)

Graduation Open House
June 2

Dear Mike,

Well, church got out late on Sunday. I didn't get too much out of the last half of the sermon. Carl says, "If the preacher is good, the preacher deserves a four-week vacation. If not, then the congregation does." We're hoping Reverend Answers will take some vacation soon.

I don't know if the congregation's on vacation, but I know our attendance has been off. Of course I usually blame the weather when attendance is down. Carl says the days are longer now because the heat expands them. And it has been hot here. Last week one day it was over eighty degrees.

It was hot in the high school auditorium last Wednesday for the graduation ceremony. The kids were uncomfortable in their caps and gowns. Carl said it was an appropriate introduction to what was ahead — sweating.

Matt Wilson was one of those sweating. It doesn't seem possible that he's already through high school. I suppose he's glad it's over. He's looking forward to his summer job on Mackinac Island at the Grand Hotel.

The last couple of weeks haven't been too easy on him. Cheryl and John had been planning an open house for Matt. It seemed like every decision was a major battle.

"Ham salad sandwiches!" Matt reacted incredulously.

"Mom, nobody serves ham salad!"

"Your grandmother and I are in charge of food," Cheryl replied curtly. No one was going to usurp her position as family festival menu planner. "Anyway, we'll have egg salad for those who don't want ham salad," she added.

"What else is on the menu?" Matt asked, resignation in his voice.

"Orange Jell-o with carrots."

"Grandma's Jell-o puts a lump in my throat," Matt responded as he left the kitchen not wanting to know what other culinary triumphs were in store.

Actually Cheryl was pleased, the conversation had ended when it did, as she didn't want to tell Matt that Bertha was baking the cake.

Bertha had insisted on baking her signature piece: pineapple upside-down cake. Even Cheryl wasn't thrilled with her mother-in-law's cake.

She'd suggested purchasing a cake so it could be frosted and have "Congratulations, Matt" written on it. But Bertha wasn't having any of it.

So Matt was in a funk — comparing his open house to those of his classmates. He'd spent a couple weeks trying to decide if there was any chance his parents would serve beer to him and his friends. He realized that was hopeless if his grandmother was catering the affair. But he'd at least hoped for hot wings, chips and salsa, food with a little bite and style, something that was profoundly lacking in his family.

Saturday afternoon was the open house. John had borrowed tables and chairs from the church. Carl, who's spending a fair amount of time up there these days, helped John load them, saying chairs are "the headquarters for hindquarters." (You can see time spent at church hasn't helped Carl.)

Out front the Wilsons had taped a banner reading "Congratulations, Matt!" to the garage door. Cheryl had arranged things in the backyard, including three display tables. One was set up with a collage of photos of Matt, starting with a few baby pictures and one from each year's school picture, from vacations, and so on. One photo showed Matt and Mike fishing, another with a new bike, prom pictures, Little League and high school baseball team pictures, and so forth.

A second table had what I suppose you'd call the mementos and awards of a teenager's life. I noticed a couple of trophies for baseball and a few certificates of achievement. There were also letters from the teachers and friends, expressing appreciation and recognizing certain success.

Those two tables flanked the table with the most interesting display I've ever seen at any open house.

Set out on this table were about fifteen or twenty things that Matt had made as gifts over the years. Here was a Christmas ornament with his photo, a clay planter painted for Cheryl on the occasion of Mother's Day, a bank made of popsicle sticks he'd given Mike after a vacation Bible school, and a few things that I wasn't sure how to classify. But all were made with loving, if unskilled, hands.

And there in the middle of that table, propped up at about a fifteen-degree angle, was the largest pineapple upside-down cake any of us had ever seen. If we hadn't eaten it, I suppose we could have called the *Guinness Book of World Records* to see if this qualified.

And more amazing than that, Bertha had spelled out with pineapple rings: "Wow, Matt."

I suppose "Congratulations, Matt" was too long even for that cake. No one wanted to cut it. But Carl said, "You can't eat your cake unless you *halve* it." I hope someone got a picture of it.

I heard Matt telling Bertha how much he enjoyed it. I'm not sure if others noticed this, but I'm sure it wasn't lost on Matt or Cheryl. If you went to the back of the cake and looked at it "wow" read "mom." I guess you could say that was a real upside-down cake.

Well, I better get this in the mail before Mr. Hurley, the mail carrier, gets here. We're praying for you and that congregation.

Love to all,
Elizabeth

Congratulations/Family/Achievement
Train children in the right way, and when old, they will not stray. (Proverbs 22:6)

A desire realized is sweet to the soul. (Proverbs 13:19a)

Carl And The Fleezehound
July 5

Dear Mike,

Well, church got out late on Sunday. I didn't get too much out of the last half of the sermon. We had a visitor who asked me, "What follows the sermon?" I was tempted to say, "Monday," but I answered, "Communion." The sermon was on prayer: "Kneeling will keep you in good standing."

Many of us have been praying for Carl, who has been hospitalized in Lansing for the better part of two weeks — kidney stones, which I gather can be very painful. I don't imagine Carl has been the best of patients, either. Coralie told us Carl said, "I have few friends in the hospital, but many enemas," or for gentler ears, "If you get run down, you wind up at the hospital." Carl tried to keep his spirits up the first few days as they tried to get him to pass the stone (or stones).

The first couple days, Carl was his usual joking self, saying he was only at stage two in his illness, the progression being ill, pill, bill, and will; and that at the hospital everyone complained about his or her condition except, of course, those with rheumatism. "They can't kick," Carl would finish the joke.

But his health wasn't a joke. And as if that weren't enough, Coralie noticed that their dog, Honduras, didn't look all that good, either. He just moped about the house and yard. Last Tuesday she took Honduras to Blair Richardson, the vet.

"How's his appetite?" Blair asked.

"He's off his feed, that's for sure," Coralie relayed. She thought of Carl's line that a man who temporarily loses his appetite is in love, and one who loses it permanently is married.

"He's missing Carl, isn't he?" she asked Blair.

"That would be my diagnosis, too," said Blair. "When's Carl coming home?"

"We don't know, probably in a few days."

"Why not run Honduras over to the hospital the next time you go. I bet it would do them both a world of good," Blair advised.

165

So Wednesday, after calling Carl to find out that he still hadn't passed the stone, was still in a great deal of pain, and that surgery was looking more attractive, Coralie and Honduras got in her car and headed to the hospital.

It never occurred to her that a family member wouldn't be allowed in the hospital. But sure enough, they were stopped at the receptionist's desk.

"No pets allowed!" the lady spoke out in no uncertain terms. Obviously, she'd been down this road before.

"And anyway, that dog doesn't look too good himself; is he sick or something?" she continued. "Can't have him in here spreading germs now, can we?"

"No, that's just the way he looks."

"I'm something of a dog fancier," the lady continued, "What exact breed is he?"

Something in her tone let it be known she only fancied fancy dogs.

Coralie found a payphone outside from which to call Carl and let him know she had to go back home to drop off Honduras and then return.

Until then, I guess Carl hadn't thought much about missing his dog. But having Honduras and Coralie so close was too much. He had Coralie walk out in the parking lot so he could see them both from his room's window. He waved and was pretty sure that Honduras looked up at his window. If there had been anyone in the room, they would have noticed the tears running down Carl's cheeks as he turned from the window. Now he was sick! And Honduras was not better for the trip, either.

That's how it was that I made a special visit to the hospital on Friday. I would have gone Thursday had I known how serious it was. But it took Henry down at Pets 'n' Stuff almost a whole day to find the harness Carl had used with Honduras in New York, and it took me most of the day to learn to walk with it.

For my part, I painted up an old cane and borrowed a pair of dark sunglasses from Matt Wilson. No hospital in America is going to keep out a seeing-eye dog and a blind woman who enjoys her independence.

What joy filled the room as Carl and Honduras were reunited. Carl was on the convalescent wing, which he said only meant "The patient is still alive," but both Honduras and Carl were so full of life during the visit you'd have thought they were home. It was just the tonic for them both. Carl passed his stone that night; Honduras went back on feed. And I shocked at least one parking lot attendant as I drove out of the lot.

Honduras and I made one last trip to the hospital on Saturday, both of us still in disguise.

"What breed of dog is that?" a woman's voice rang out from beyond the reception desk.

"Oh, um, ah, he's a Fleezehound," I replied in a burst of inspiration.

"I'm seeing more of them all the time. Do they make pretty good leader dogs?" she queried.

"You'd be hard pressed to find a better breed, they know how to look up," I said, wildly waving my cane over my head, to demonstrate my point as I made my way to the bank of elevators. I thought to myself, "and they can see without looking and look without seeing."

Coralie decided to put on the dog, so to speak, for Carl's return. She went so far as to talk of getting Honduras a new doghouse. "Big enough," she says, "for a large dog or a small man." I'd say life is pretty well back to normal for them all.

Well, I'd better get this in the mail before Mr. Hurley, the mail carrier, gets here. We're praying for you and your congregation.

Love to all,
Elizabeth

Look up
Seek the Lord and his strength; seek his presence continually.
(Psalm 105:4)

The New Cookbook
September 1

Dear Mike,

Well, church got out late on Sunday. I didn't get too much out of the last half of the sermon. What is it Carl says? "The difference between an audience and a congregation is an audience listens and a congregation doesn't." I will say that this August more than ever I've been in favor of air conditioning the church. They say it is unhealthy to sleep in stuffy rooms.

T. S. Eliot may believe April is the cruelest month, but I'm here to say it is August — at least for those of us who still enter items to be judged at the county fair. And this August was the worst ever for me as I was completely shut out of the ribbons in every category. Of course, there's a good reason why, but here I am, getting ahead of myself.

In late July, I did my usual accounting in the cellar. As I plan out what I'm going to put up, I always take my cookbook down with me. That way I can look at the recipes and see, for example, if I'm putting up the 24 pints of bread-and-butter pickles, how much vinegar or sugar I'll be needing, doing the math and making notes as I go.

At any rate, as I was checking the shelves the phone rang, so I hurried back upstairs. In the conversation with Coralie I forgot all about my precious cookbook still in the basement. I think I'm about up to Z in Alzheimer's already.

A few days later when I needed to look up a recipe, I went back downstairs looking for it and got the shock of my life. It was gone! And I mean gone!

Well, perhaps recycled is a more accurate description. A field mouse evidently decided my cookbook would make ideal nesting material and had literally torn it to shreds. I believe it would have been a more fitting end if the mouse had just eaten it.

Carl said you don't usually think of a cookbook as a book with an unhappy ending. But this was much more than a cookbook. It was my history book. I'd kept it since I was a teenager.

And it was gone. Several of my mother's recipes were in it, written in her hand, including her birthday cake with caramel icing, something I still make and, fortunately, have entrusted to memory by now.

Also gone were my Pillsbury Bake Off recipes. These are the recipes that over the years people have told me, "This is the best I've ever eaten!" or "I must have the recipe for this, Elizabeth." Now you know I've never won with any of them, and, at first, I was quite disappointed with the judges' lack of discernment. Now, of course, I've come to realize that Pillsbury was using the same judges that McDonald's has been using for their Monopoly game.

How well I still recall my first rejection letter on a sour cream cake. (Mike, you've eaten that cake yourself and told me how good it was.) I was so agitated that, quick as a wink, I whipped up some basic white bread dough and fashioned a Pillsbury doughboy.

"Into the fiery furnace," I said as I put him into the 350-degree oven.

Once done and cool enough to handle he was drawn and quartered, with butter. But not before I'd bitten his head off.

And now, Mike, I'd not only lost the sour cream cake recipe, but the basic white bread recipe, too. You can see why I cried for two days.

Of course, many of the recipes I'd used for the county fair were lost as well, including the aforementioned bread-and-butter pickles. Most of the fair entries I'd made notations on with the date or dates entered and which ribbon, if any, they'd won. The list of things I lost could fill, well — a cookbook.

Coralie actually got me on the road to recovery. She stopped by the following Saturday with a pecan coffee cake, which I realized was a recipe of mine. Along with it she'd brought the recipe and, surprisingly, about thirty more, she'd gotten from me over time.

That Sunday, she put out the word at church asking for people who had recipes they'd gotten from me to make copies and return them. On Monday, she put the word out through town. Rex, the cook at the Busy-Bee said he had over forty, which I'm sure is an exaggeration. However, it is nice to have the recognition of your peers. I'd say half a dozen former 4-H kids brought recipes from when I taught cooking and nutrition skills.

Well, by the end of the month, it was worse than having your name at the top of a chain letter. And if truth be told many of the recipes I was receiving weren't mine to begin with. But what a tribute, that I was considered author or creator of so many good recipes. (And a few duds.) I actually believe I ended up with more than I started with.

Coralie bought me a new notebook and Carl printed up a cover that said "Seasoned With Love." Yes, I cried for two more days. And yes, I got my basic white bread recipe back. And if you're wondering, I couldn't resist baking up another Pillsbury doughboy.

When he'd cooled enough, I grasped him firmly in my hand and said rather calmly, "Now I've got you, and now I'm gonna eat you," and with those words I bit off his head, drew and quartered him, and slathered him with butter.

Anyway, by the time I'd rebuilt the cookbook, the deadline for the fair had long passed, so I had to content myself with dreaming about next year.

Well, I'd better get this in the mail before Mr. Hurley, the mail carrier, gets here. We're praying for you and your congregation.

Love to all,
Elizabeth

Cast bread upon waters
Send out your bread upon the waters, for after many days you will get it back. (Ecclesiastes 11:1)

Shotgun
October 4

Dear Mike,

Well, church got out late on Sunday. I didn't get too much out of the last half of the sermon. Carl says Reverend Answers gets it trite the first time. But I admit it isn't easy for Reverend Answers. He's got a congregation that wants the front of the plane, the back of the church, and the middle of the road.

The kids have all gone back to school. The Johnsons' youngest, Cara, started kindergarten. When she got home, her mom, Louise, asked her if she'd learned anything. Cara replied, "Well, not enough; that's why I have got to go back tomorrow."

Fall is finally here in full color. We're all trying to get the last few things out of our gardens. I'm pleased with the way my tomatoes have produced. The beefsteaks are about gone, but the others are still doing well. Carl says I ought to quit bragging on my garden, and plant more radishes and cucumbers ... they speak for themselves.

This is a wonderful time of year around here. We're all busy getting things ready for our Fall Harvest Bazaar. I've signed up for apple butter again this year. But I had way more apples than I could possibly use.

I encouraged the Wilson boys, Matt and Mike, to use some of the Romes and Winesaps to press cider. What is it Carl says? "Cider is the hardest part of the apple."

Well, I guess the boys spent all of the last couple weeks rounding up glass jugs, getting my old press working and collecting the apples, and pressing the cider.

I'm not sure where they got the idea, but one of them thought they might put aside a couple of jugs to "ripen." Matt quoted Carl, saying, "Adam would have been better off if he'd drunk the apple rather than eaten it." I guess drunk was what they had in mind.

Anyway, they set aside some, finally deciding on George and Bertha's basement fruit cellar as the ideal place to stash it.

I heard Mildred Warren say to her students: "If an alarm clock won't make you rise, try yeast," but I doubt if I ever expected to hear of it working. Thursday night, it did just that.

Bertha and George were awakened by an explosion somewhere in the basement. One of the jugs had reached its tensile limit of eighty pounds per square inch pressure.

The shock of hearing a gun go off in their house really had them awake. Bertha told George there was a burglar in the house sure as anything, and to call the police.

George SHSHHHed her and got his shotgun from the closet. "I'll take care of this," he whispered.

Rather than turn on the lights and alert the intruder, George made his way downstairs from the bedroom. He thought he heard something in the dining room and sure enough, when he slipped into the room he saw some movement on the far side of the room. He lifted the shotgun to his shoulder and was about to say something when he noticed a gun being pointed in his direction by a dark figure. He fired. Most of George's shooting has been limited to pool and bull, so it's understandable that things didn't go well.

He'd actually shot his own reflection in the mirror on Bertha's bowfront. The damage to her Depression glass was as complete as it was swift.

The shattering glass brought Bertha running from upstairs. She expected the worst: George shot and lying on the floor. What she found was worse: her bowfront and glass collection blown to smithereens. George was lucky he'd discharged both barrels. Bertha took the gun from him.

"Who shot first?" she asked sarcastically.

"Well, at least I scared off the intruder," George said rather gamely, considering.

"How'd he get out? The same way he got in?" She wasn't going to be put off.

The next morning Bertha made a clean sweep of the house. She threw out all of George's shotgun shells. In the process she discovered the broken glass jug and spilled cider in the fruit cellar. She called Matt and Mike in for a little talking to.

Of course, by noon everyone at the Busy-Bee Café had heard about it. Carl told George he was going to start calling him Tylenol, he's such a good pane killer. Jokes aside, it was a pretty sobering experience for Matt, Mike, and George.

Well, I'd better get this in the mail before Mr. Hurley, the mail carrier, gets here. We're praying for you and your congregation.

Love to all,
Elizabeth

Treasure in heaven
But store up for yourselves treasures in heaven, where neither moth nor rust consumes and where thieves do not break in and steal. (Matthew 6:20)

Dear Mike,

Well, church got out late on Sunday. I didn't get too much out of the last half of the sermon. Sometimes it is hard to hear what Reverend Answers is saying; unfortunately, that wasn't the case Sunday. The sermon was like a bad tooth — the longer it was drawn out, the more painful it was. Next Sunday Reverend Answers will be away. Carl jokes, "We're planning a service of praise and singing."

We had our first snow of the season, about three inches. It didn't last too long, but it did do a good job of knocking the leaves off the trees. I think most of the people around here were sorry to see the leaves go as they were spectacular this year.

At least two people weren't sorry to see them go, however. Beauty has never figured too heavily in Ernest Porter's life, if you ask me. He lives a pretty spartan existence. And, it seems, the joy in his life comes from politics, or at least talking politics down at the Busy-Bee Café.

Now I won't say people take pains to avoid him, but during October and early November, Darlene swears her tips are off 20%.

There are several people who do take pains to avoid him. Jim Hesler is one. You may recall that the Hesler house backs up to Porters' farm. There is a small wood lot — I'd guess about twenty acres between the two places, and therein lies the reason Jim avoids Ernest.

Three, no it was four years ago, Ernest was out in back of his house and heard a chainsaw in the woods, which he owns. Upon investigation, he found Jim buzzing up firewood from a couple of windfalls.

"That's my wood!" Ernest said to a startled Jim.

"No, I think this is on my property," replied Jim.

"It most certainly is not! How can you be so stupid? I own the whole lot," Ernest continued in the vein that wins him all those friends.

"Not according to my deed. Twenty feet of the woods is on my lot," Jim replied.

"Well, get off until it's settled. Stealing wood! If you needed wood, you should have just come and asked."

"And given you the joy of saying, 'No' — never!" was Jim's final remark as he turned and left the woods.

The survey showed that Jim had about ten feet of woods, but where he was cutting was definitely Porter's property.

Ernest hauled the wood to his house where, I guess, it's still stacked. Ernest tells anyone who will listen, "All he has to do is ask for it and I'll *give* it to him."

So they haven't spoken in four years, perhaps a blessing in disguise for Jim, at least at election time.

But this isn't to say they haven't communicated. And, in fact, that's why they both were looking forward to the leaves being off the trees. You see, they're both under the mistaken notion there's a big barn owl living in one of those trees.

Early last summer, Jim was out in his garden about dusk doing a little hoeing when he heard what he thought was an owl's hoot. At about the same time Ernest had ventured off his back porch toward the garage and he heard something.

Both men stopped stock still and listened. Jim hooted to see if he could get a response — "whooo."

"Whooo," came back the reply from Ernest.

"Whooo, whooo," howled Jim.

"Whooo, whooo," came back Ernest.

The next day, Jim was at the library looking up *Peterson's Guide to North America's Birds*. Ernest didn't need the library. He knew a barn owl when he heard one.

Most evenings just at dusk you could find the two of them in their respective backyards — "Whoo-whooing" each other, both engaging in some pretty fancy hoots, trills, calls, and runs. And invariably getting the same birdsong echoing back through the woods. Jim has gone so far as to think the bird was a cross between an owl and a mockingbird.

So both men were pleased that the snow had brought down most of the leaves and they could perhaps get a glimpse of their invisible interlocutor.

In fact, both men ventured into the wood lot from opposite sides about a quarter after five last Tuesday. Being preoccupied with looking heavenward, neither noticed the other moving toward him. They were less than twenty yards apart before Jim noticed Ernest. (It was getting dark, and they were trying not to disturb the owl.)

When Jim saw Ernest's head pitched back, giving his best owl imitation, he realized immediately what had been going on all summer. There was no owl, just two old coots.

"What do I do?" wondered Jim, "let Ernest go on thinking there was an owl here, which vanishes tonight, come clean and let him know how we've been fooling ourselves, or perhaps have a little more fun by stringing him along?"

It was pretty dark when Jim got back to his house. "Did you find the owl?" Martha asked.

"No, it's a couple of loons," he replied.

Well, I'd better get this in the mail before Mr. Hurley, the mail carrier, gets here. We're praying for you and your congregation.

Love to all,
Elizabeth

Living as good neighbors
How very good and pleasant it is when kindred live together in unity! (Psalm 133:1)

Do not seek your own advantage, but that of the other. (1 Corinthians 10:24)

Dear Mike,

Well, church got out late on Sunday. I didn't get too much out of the last half of the sermon. Carl says with Reverend Answers, talk is cheap. Of course, that's always the case when supply exceeds demand. Carl says, "Reverend Answers speaks without a note," but Carl is quick to add, "and without a point." But if truth be told, I didn't get much out of the first half of the sermon either. I was home with the flu.

What is it Carl says? "The flu has both an affirmative and a negative. Sometimes the eyes have it, sometimes the nose." I guess it's going around the school as well. I heard that Karen Kohler missed last week with it. It wasn't the flu; perhaps it was a bad case of embarrassment.

She invited Curt Bridges over for Thanksgiving dinner again this year. Curt, you may recall, coaches and teaches drivers' ed. They seem to be thrown together often at the high school where they teach, I suppose by virtue of being single. But also because many of us think they'd be a perfect couple.

Last year when Karen invited Curt over for Thanksgiving, I think she hoped it might be the beginning of something more serious than being senior prom chaperones. She really outdid herself for the meal and in decorating her house. (She's sort of the town's answer to Martha Stewart.) So you can imagine her disappointment when, after the meal, Curt asked to turn on the television to watch football. He watched for what seemed like hours, and she cleaned up the kitchen and packed Curt some leftovers with preprinted warming instructions — did I mention Martha Stewart? Then she tried to get interested in the game.

"Is that guy a contortionist?" she asked in her most naive voice, with only a hint of sarcasm. "I mean the announcer just said he ran around his own end."

This year Karen felt she understood her quarry a little better and took steps to prevent a repeat of last year's football follies.

On Monday, she brought home a media cart from school and loaded her television on it. She then wheeled it into her sewing room. She actually liked the look of the living room better without the television and was considering buying a cart to wheel it from room to room after the holidays; something she won't need now, of course, but I'm getting ahead of myself.

"After all," she mused, "you never see a television in any of the photographs in *Martha Stewart Living*."

It was a feast for two that she prepared: turkey with chestnut dressing, glazed yams, winter greens from her garden, sparkling cider, and pears with cheese. "Every bite more delicious than the last," according to Curt. Karen had to admit that one of Curt's most attractive features was his appetite. He ate enough for two or three people and thoroughly enjoyed every morsel.

But after the meal, his least attractive feature reared its ugly head.

"Where's your television?" he asked. "You know the Lions are playing."

"It's broken," she lied, thinking that was the easiest way to avoid a repeat of last Thanksgiving.

"I'll go get my tools and take a look at it," he said, hopping up from the table and out the front door to his pickup before she could voice a protest.

Quick as a wink, Karen was in the sewing room. With the strength that only comes from a half a pint of adrenaline coursing through one's veins, she lifted the television off the cart and dropped it to the floor. She hoped Curt didn't hear the ensuing crash.

"You weren't joking when you said it was broken," he said, surveying the scene in the sewing room. "I doubt if I can fix that; in fact, I doubt if anyone can."

"I'm surprised you haven't picked up the pieces," he continued.

"Well, it only recently happened," Karen explained, edging past him and drawing them both back into the living room.

"Why don't we go down to Gallagher's and catch the game there?" Curt suggested.

"I'm sure they're not open on Thanksgiving. Let's just stay here and talk," Karen offered.

178

"Oh, I know they're open," Curt said. "I've spent many a Thanksgiving there."

"You're kidding, right?" She asked with hope fading from her voice. "I mean, who goes in there?" Karen wondered if there were any women in the tavern. Her image was of a dark, dank, smelly place with knotty wood paneling, none of which held any appeal.

"Do they serve women?" she asked, showing another of her misconceptions.

"No, you have to bring your own," Curt replied, trying to lighten the mood. "Grab your coat."

"Are there any women at all?" Karen persisted.

"Well, let's see, Darlene's usually there and Wanda Dolan, the school cook, what's her name, and Elizabeth, to name just a few," he told her. She obliged him rather than sit at home and brood over the fact that she didn't have a television to watch.

Karen was surprised to find Gallagher's full as Curt had predicted. If truth be told, about half of the town's singles were there. The mood was warm, the chance to gab was great, and the Lions maintained their losing record: 0 and 9.

Curt got to watch his football; Karen got to mingle and get the feel of the true Gallagher's, and I got the flu bug. At least that's where I suspect I picked it up.

The next day, Curt showed up unannounced at Karen's midmorning with a package. He'd gotten up early to drive over to Lansing to shop on what Curt could attest to as the busiest shopping day of the year.

"I thought you could use this," Curt said, bringing the box into the living room.

Karen, judging from the box, assumed it was a mirror or painting.

"I can't believe it's a television," she gasped as she opened the box.

"Not just a television," Curt corrected. "This is an HDTV, the latest technology, virtually unbreakable. You see, you can mount it on the wall. Hang it like a picture," Curt explained. "If it falls, nothing to break," he continued.

Once he had it installed and plugged it in, Karen was thrilled. "You'll have to stay for dinner," Karen insisted.

"Is there anything on television?" she asked.

"Football," Curt replied.

"Football, is it on seven days a week now?" she worried aloud. To her credit, Karen resisted the urge to tear the screen from the wall and test just how unbreakable it might actually be.

"You know, I think you'd enjoy football if you understood it. Let me explain it," Curt offered, settling comfortably into the couch.

"Well, he does have a good appetite," Karen thought as she dropped back into the kitchen.

Well, I'd better get this in the mail before Mr. Hurley, the mail carrier, gets here. We're praying for you and your church.

Love to all,
Elizabeth

Deceit
The heart is devious above all else, it is perverse — who can understand it? (Jeremiah 17:9)

So then, putting away falsehood, let all of us speak the truth to our neighbors, for we are members of one another. (Ephesians 4:25)

Section 5:
Last Year

Maze
January 2

Dear Mike,

Well, church got out late on Sunday. I didn't get too much out of the last half of the sermon. There's never a dull moment at church — more like a half an hour. Just once I'd like for Reverend Answers to sit in the congregation, what Carl calls the windward side of the chancel.

Speaking of wind, we've had our share of it lately. What is it Carl says? "It's been so cold even the wind is howling about it." Between Christmas and New Year's we had a blizzard, a snowstorm, not a day where the temperature got above freezing, overcast skies, and drifting snow — and that was just the first day. We've recorded more snow in December than we did for all of last winter. Some are saying this is the worst winter since 1978, and I believe they're right.

Not everyone is complaining about the weather, though. It has given at least a couple of people in town an opportunity to realize longtime dreams. Blaine Richardson closed down the Refrigerator Magnet Museum during the holidays for two weeks. A couple of years ago, he had a tractor out plowing the snow in the parking lot, and just for fun, he began making some designs as the snow was pushed up, leaving paths. Blaine, who never was what anyone would call a straight thinker, had an absolute rabbit's warren of pathways cleared through the snow on the lot. That night, he thought it might be fun to construct a maze out in the parking lot. Of course, the last two years haven't provided him with the actual building material: snow.

But it was already over three feet deep in places when he put the word out to friends, people in town, employees, and summer help to come for a day of winter fun. And Mike, surprisingly, it was fun! Blaine opened the museum for us to warm up in. The snack bar served free food all day and people worked like crazy.

Blaine's idea was to construct walls about eight feet high from snow blocks that were formed in the rectangular metal trash cans they have at the museum. All day blocks were formed in the molds, and set into place on Blaine's design. Blaine gave it a final spray of water to mortar it all together. And it is rock solid after all this cold!

What fun we had finding our way through it. It is deceptively difficult because many of the passages are so narrow and many of the openings are 45-degree angle slits where two walls meet. At the end of the day we'd constructed a sixty-foot square maze, and surprisingly, cleared most of the Refrigerator Magnet Museum's parking lot of snow. Tell me Blaine isn't a genius.

Over the next three days, it got fairly good use and each day Blaine and Matt Wilson would go out and patch it up just after dawn — and although they deny it, I think, change it around. At least I had trouble making my way through it on Friday, and I can't believe I couldn't remember my way around. But the pure white walls are deceptive.

New Year's Eve, Matt Wilson had a date with Leia Axner. Theirs is an on-again, off-again relationship. It seems to heat up as the weather cools, and then cools off each summer as the weather heats up. They'd gone to the Hollister girls' New Year's Eve party, but Matt and Leia had left about 11:00, as Matt wanted to spend some time alone with Leia, mostly in the hopes of getting some idea of where their relationship was going.

He'd decided it would be fun to stroll through the maze, time it just right for a kiss at midnight and "ring in the new year." Life seldom runs as planned. The maze, which is difficult during the day, proved downright impossible at night, although they had the maze to themselves. It was way too cold for lingering, much less romance. After about five minutes, Leia was ready to go. Unfortunately, they couldn't find the exit.

"It can't be too much farther; let's try again," Matt offered in his cheeriest voice.

"I think that's the third time you've said that," Leia said icily.

"You know I learned to ride a two-wheeler in one of these," Matt said, trying to change the subject, but embarrassed he'd used a child's word "two-wheeler."

"I know how you learned to stop," Leia answered, "but how'd you learn to turn?" And wondered to herself exactly how fit John and Cheryl were as parents.

"When I was four, I got a bicycle for Christmas but I couldn't ride it because of the snow, cold weather, and perhaps more importantly, Dad couldn't find the training wheels. But Dad shoveled the snow off the driveway and would run alongside of me as I rode. But I couldn't stay up without him running by me. And I guess he lost interest in that method after about twenty trips back and forth."

"Is this story going someplace?" Leia sighed mostly to herself, a little puff of breath showing in the cold.

"Well, the next day," Matt continued, "Dad got out the snowblower, cut a swath in the snow in the backyard. It was more like a snow trench, just barely wide enough for the bike and me."

"How did you stop?" Leia asked, going back to her original image of Matt riding into a snow bank.

"I didn't have to; it was a big circle," Matt replied.

"I don't know that it really held me up, but when I fell over, it was only about a foot, and then it was into snow," he continued.

Now the question on her mind wasn't is the story going someplace, *but are we?* "Are we going to have to dig our way out of here or climb over the wall?" Leia asked, a sense of urgency now in her voice.

"Stand here," Matt said. "Put your arms on the wall." With that he dropped down, hoisted her up on his shoulders.

Leia's head was now above the walls.

"Go forward, now left, now right." She began reeling off directions faster than Matt could keep up.

"Left again, one more," she continued. Now that she could see the silhouetted entrance and passageways she was in no hurry to get out. Right, no, left, no, straight.

He lowered her a few steps from the exit. The snow blanketing everything made it so quiet Matt was sure he could hear his heart beat, which I might add, was racing, and not from exertion.

They kissed. Matt was sure it was right at the stroke of midnight. He knew this was going to be an amazing year.

Well, I'd better get this in the mail before Mr. Hurley, the mail carrier, gets here. We're praying for you and your congregation.

Love to all,
Elizabeth

Guidance/Perspective
... he restores my soul. He leads me in right paths for his name's sake. (Psalm 23:3)

Electric Blanket
February 3

Dear Mike,

Well, church got out late on Sunday. I didn't get too much out of the last half of the sermon. Carl says, "Our church has them standing in line — to get out." I will say Reverend Answers can speak for an hour without a note, and alas, without a point.

If the truth be told, I believe everyone's mind was on the weather. You've probably seen on the news the reports of the terrible snow and ice storms we've been having the last ten days or so. Carl said it was so cold he saw Ernest Porter at the Busy-Bee Café with his toupee on upside down.

The real hardship isn't the cold, of course, but rather the damage from the ice storms. How something so beautiful on the trees and the crest of the snow can do so much damage is a mystery to me. But sure enough, the roads were so slick several people skidded off into ditches. I didn't even venture down to my mailbox one day, doubting if Mr. Hurley had even gotten this far out in his deliveries and doubting if I'd make it back to the house.

But the worst is the inevitable power outages as tree limbs snap under the weight of the ice and the wind takes down electrical lines.

Our problem out here is trying to get the power restored. We labor under at least two burdens that relate to the town's name. When a cartographer draws up a map and writes "Maybe," the typographer and printer see that as a cartographer's note rather than a place name, which means you won't find Maybe on many of the state-produced highway maps.

The other reason is like unto it. When we call into the electric company in Lansing to report an outage, it is entered into the computer as: "Power Outage, Maybe" which the lineman, unless he's familiar with this part of the grid, ignores until a confirmation comes along. Obviously, it is impossible for the worker to confirm the place looking at a state-produced map.

All of this means that what might be a couple of hours of inconvenience some place down the line, for us can be two or three days. Carl always tries to lighten the mood with his old saw, "You can't fuel all of the people all of the time." Usually that doesn't help. Even before the storms hit, the Wilson boys, Matt and Mike, had tried their best to winterize their grandparents' house. The grandsons are worried about Bertha's health each winter because she gets so sick with colds and the flu. She and George always get the immunization shots. Matt said they've been to the doctor so often they just back in to save time.

Last Christmas, the boys bought George and Bertha a beautiful claret-colored electric blanket in the hopes that it would keep them healthier. In March, they were disappointed to find it still in the box, unused. George promised they'd use it this winter. To ensure that it did get used, Matt and Mike went over to their grandparents' to set them up for winter with one main purpose.

After helping change the furnace filters, stacking wood for the wood burning stove, and getting some sweaters unpacked, the boys made the bed with the new electric blanket and flannel sheets. Mike said it was too bad they didn't have a mint to put on each pillow.

I guess George and Bertha actually looked forward to trying out the new electric blanket with the individual controls that night. You know, it was sort of a new experience for them. So when they got in bed each one set their control on "5." I understand the controls went from low "0" to "9" high.

George is kind of cold by nature and Bertha hot, so it wasn't too long before they were each reaching for their respective controls. George thought maybe a "6" would be a little toastier, while Bertha thought a "3" might suit her. They drifted off. But not for long. George woke up cold ... well, maybe "8"; Bertha woke up in a sweat ... well, maybe a "1." George was really getting cold ... I wonder if I there's anything above "9"?

Bertha got up and opened the window. George woke up in a draft. He couldn't believe it. He made his way down the hall to the thermostat. He'd show Bertha; he'd turn up the furnace. As he reached for the thermostat, he remembered Reverend Answers saying in a sermon, "If you want to get even with someone, get even with a favor they've done for you."

He slowly made his way back to the bedroom. "Well, at least I'm going to shut that window," he thought to himself. As he rounded the corner of the bed he put his hand down to steady himself. It was hot. Very hot! Probably a "9." George realized the controls were switched. He'd been turning up Bertha's side and she'd been turning his down.

He closed the window, unplugged the electric blanket, and got an extra quilt out of the closet for his side of the bed. They awoke snuggled up in the middle.

George says they're getting used to the electric blanket now and may even plug it in again once the electricity comes back on.

Well, I'd better get this in the mail before Mr. Hurley, the mail carrier, gets here. Yes, he's been making his rounds, albeit a bit slower than usual. We're praying for you and your congregation.

Love to all,
Elizabeth

Interrelatedness/One another
And let us consider how to provoke one another to love and good deeds. (Hebrews 10:24)

For this is the message you have heard from the beginning, that we should love one another. (1 John 3:11)

Dear Mike,

Well, church got out late on Sunday. I didn't get too much out of the last half of the sermon. Reverend Answers puts words in our ears and faith in our patience. Carl said it was a "steer sermon" — "A point here, a point there, and lots of bull in between." But I doubt if Reverend Answers would have minded the criticism. Things are going well at home and at church these days.

A couple of weeks ago, he had a wedding at church for Thelma's son and his fiancée. While waiting for the pictures after the wedding, Reverend Answers made his way out to the front of the church where the biggest limousine he'd ever seen was waiting for the newlyweds.

"You know, I've never seen the inside of one of those," Reverend Answers told the driver, hoping to get a peek.

"Climb in the back, Padre," the driver offered, opening the door.

"Wow, this is huge!" Reverend Answers enthused, sliding across the half-acre of leather.

"Oh, yeah, this one comes equipped with a walk-in glove box," the driver quipped through the open door.

"How much does it cost to rent something like this?" Reverend Answers asked from the leather backseat.

"Well, it's supply and demand. Fridays and Saturdays, about $150 per hour with a four-hour minimum. On Valentine's Day," he continued, "it's $250 per hour."

What is it Carl says? "Valentine's Day is the day for heart attacks."

"Well, that's why I've never been in one," Reverend Answers concluded, considering the cost.

"You interested in a rental?" the driver asked. "If you want to go out this Tuesday night, it's $50 an hour."

"Still a little steep," Reverend Answers replied. But the idea of Peggy and him riding around the country in a limo had a certain appeal.

"Tell you what, let me bring my old lady, and I'll split the cost 40/60 with you."

Reverend Answers was shocked when Peggy didn't seem as thrilled with the idea.

"You say I'm never spontaneous," he whined. "Now you know why. I'm not encouraged in it."

"Bob, there's a thin line between spontaneity and stupidity," she answered. "Don't make me draw that line for you. Think what the church people would say if a limo pulled up in front of the parsonage to pick us up. I thought you were hoping for a raise. People will think we've got money to burn."

Reverend Answers decided he'd wait to break the news about Wendel, the driver, bringing his "old lady." If truth be told, Reverend Answers wasn't sure if Wendel had meant his mother, his girlfriend, or his wife. But he did figure if they met the limo out on the highway at the Chevron station, no one in town would be the wiser.

"I'm just doing this to humor you," Peggy announced at breakfast that day. But by then, she was looking forward to cruising around seeing without being seen for four hours that evening. "Where are we going, anyway?"

"We've got a small detour," Reverend Answers told Wendel as they got into the limo at the Chevron station.

"One of our members is in the hospital in Lansing," he continued. "We'll need to go there first."

Gladys had had a stroke that morning and Taylor had called Reverend Answers from the Lansing Hospital in the early afternoon. Gladys was still in a coma, and the doctors weren't sure how extensive the stroke was.

"I'm glad you're not dressed like a padre today. People sure would wonder what church you're from," Wendel said as Reverend Answers got out of the limo at the hospital entrance.

"I'll only be a few minutes."

Gladys had been moved from emergency to a room in intensive care. Ron and Sherry were there with Taylor. They took turns looking in on her but weren't able to notice any real sign of mental alertness. Their faces told of their concern.

191

Taylor told Reverend Answers to come back to her room with him.

"Darling, it's me, Taylor, who loves you." With that, he bent over and kissed her. "Honey, look who's here to see you," Taylor announced Reverend Answers' arrival. Reverend Answers said a prayer and then sat with the family for a while.

When he left the hospital, Wendel pulled the limo out to meet him.

"Get in the front seat," Wendel called through the half-opened passenger window.

Reverend Answers noted that Wendel's "old lady" was in the backseat, and she and Peggy were engaged in an animated conversation.

"Where to, Padre?"

With that, Reverend Answers began a route he'd been working out in his mind the previous three days.

Reverend Answers and Wendel had quite a conversation about the limo, the owners, Wendel's experiences as a driver, and so on.

"What's it like to drive something this big?" Reverend Answers asked.

"Like piloting a ship," Wendel replied, grinning.

After a long pause, Reverend Answers popped the question. "How about letting me drive for a while?"

"Against company policy."

"Well, you don't look like a by-the-book kind of guy. Is it in the book for the driver to bring along a date?" Reverend Answers used the term "date," having only ruled out one of the three possible definitions of "old lady."

"Just don't break any laws," Wendel said, as he traded seats with Reverend Answers.

"Could I wear the hat and jacket, too?" excitement rising in his voice.

And she says I'm not spontaneous, Reverend Answers mused to himself as he nosed the limo into the Chevron parking lot at the end of the night.

As luck would have it, the Lockwoods were gassing up at the time the limo arrived.

"Look over there," Rob said to Joan, motioning with his head and hiding behind the pump.

"Is it someone famous?" Joan asked excitedly, eyeing the limo.

"Not the passenger," Rob said. "Look at the driver. Don't let him see you." And, in fact, Reverend Answers didn't see the Lockwoods.

I suppose no one was more surprised than Reverend Answers at Wednesday's board meeting, when they voted him a raise of $3,000 for the rest of the year, with the proviso that he did not take any outside work.

Well, I'd better get this in the mail before Mr. Hurley, the mail carrier, gets here. We're praying for you and your congregation.

Love to all,
Elizabeth

Trust
The Lord will keep your going out and your coming in from this time on and forevermore. (Psalm 121:8)

High School Graduation
June 3

Dear Mike,

Well, church got out late on Sunday. I didn't get too much out of the last half of the sermon. Reverend Answers took his time in the sermon. Of course, he took ours, too. Carl said that Reverend Answers is outspoken. But I'd like to know by whom. We're thinking of suggesting the offering be renamed "hush money."

Mike Wilson graduated from high school last week. The commencement was Tuesday. Mike and a friend had decided a couple of weeks ago that they were going out in style. They had plotted their prank down to the last detail. But like most plans, things didn't turn out exactly as plotted. What is it Carl says? "A plan is either something abandoned or unfinished."

Mike had unlocked one of the windows in the Sunday school wing of the church so he and Billy could slip into the church on Monday night and hang a banner from the spire of the church. The banner read, "Look up, Seniors!" which could be interpreted a couple of ways.

They slipped into the church about midnight and made their way to the stairs that led to the belfry's trapdoor. They were armed with flashlights and had picked up the stepladder from the janitor's closet. When Mike poked his head through the trapdoor, he got the shock of his life. There staring back at him was a bear.

He tumbled back down into Billy's arms.

"There's a *bear* up there," he blurted out in a half whisper, half shout.

"A what?" asked Billy, realizing the unlikelihood of a bear in the belfry.

They retreated to the church basement to figure their next move.

"Are you sure?" Billy asked for about the third time.

"You want to look for yourself?" countered Mike.

"Well, think about it. How could it live up there? What does it eat?" Billy continued.

"How about stupid seniors?"

"Boy, they sure don't want anybody up there," Billy observed. "Well, what are we going to do?" Billy continued.

How the bear came to reside in the belfry is an interesting story. You may recall how a couple of years ago at Easter, Reverend Answers released homing pigeons during the children's sermon. Unbeknownst to us, one mating pair took up residence in the belfry and soon caused a nuisance. Twice Mr. Sorda, the birds' owner, came to remove them and their brood, and twice they returned "home."

Carl had mentioned the problem to Henry from Pets 'n' Stuff. What is it Carl says? "Henry really knows his stuff." Henry said he thought he had a solution. He suggested taking the old bear from the store to the church belfry to act as a deterrent to the pigeons. So there it was in its most fearsome pose, reared up on its hind legs, paws raised, jaws agape. Of course, no could see it from the ground.

I guess it did the job, as we haven't had any problem with pigeons since. Now I can't say whether there is a direct connection or not, but some of the Sorda racing pigeons have been doing exceptionally well lately. I don't know if they're from the brood that was born at the church or not, but I'd like to think so. And I believe I have some justification for that belief.

Last week Mr. Sorda sent eight birds to Wisconsin for a 400-mile race. Actually, for most birds it's maybe 600 miles. According to Mr. Sorda, that race goes not to the swift, not to the strongest, not to even the smartest. It goes to the birds with the most faith, which supports my theory very nicely, thank you. "Faith," you say? Consider.

The shortest route for the birds is across Lake Michigan. But land birds don't like to fly across bodies of water where they can't see the opposite shore. It makes sense, of course; if they get out there and get tired, there aren't a lot of landing options. And, of course, they've never crossed it, so they don't know how wide the lake is. Most of the birds end up flying the shore route south, which adds about 200 miles to the race. Near Chicago, the lake is narrow enough for them to get back on track.

Six of Sorda's birds took the direct route home. They were rewarded for their faith as they were all in the top ten finishing in Saturday's race. All clocked-in in less than eight hours.

Tuesday morning most of the town was greeted to an unusual sight. The bear was about halfway out of the belfry (top half). The banner, now abridged, was unfurled from one paw. "Look up" was crossed out and in its place was "Bear down, Seniors." Of course, most of the town was wondering not who, but how they got the bear up there.

Carl says, "Graduation is the end of study and the beginning of an education." Of course, he's also the one who said Tuesday morning at the Busy-Bee, "Go hunting bear, and you're liable to catch cold."

Well, I'd better get this in the mail before Mr. Hurley, the mail carrier, gets here. We're praying for you and your congregation.

Love to all,
Elizabeth

Faith
Now faith is the assurance of things hoped for, the conviction of things not seen. (Hebrews 11:1)

Lost Sense Of Smell
July 3

Dear Mike,

Well, church got out late on Sunday. I didn't get too much out of the last half of the sermon. Some of Reverend Answers' sermons are like water to a drowning man. Carl said, "Some work from sun to sun, but Reverend Answers' word is never done. Here it is almost the Fourth of July and his tongue never gets a holiday. I'm surprised he doesn't get sunburn on it."

Speaking of sunburn, have you noticed the new UV rating for each part of the country? Carl says, "Ignorance is blister," so this may help. I see from the news it's been hot out your way. The weather forecaster said it was 117 degrees in the shade in Phoenix. Don't be a fool, Mike; stay in the sun.

We've all been trying to take it easy. I notice a lot of people using their porches in the evening. The mosquitoes haven't been too bad this year. What is it Carl says? "Mosquitoes are like people. They don't get a slap on the back until they go to work."

Last Tuesday night, the Lockwoods were out enjoying their porch. They'd closed the hardware store at 8 o'clock, but there were still a couple of hours of daylight, and they were out front enjoying the coolness. The lilacs by the house are still in bloom, and they added an unmistakable fragrance to the evening air.

Mr. Hurley, the mail carrier, who just lives up the street, was out for his evening constitutional. Mr. Hurley walks most evenings. His delivery is a rural route, so unlike some of the mail carriers, he doesn't get much exercise on the job — unless stretching across the front seat of a car and hanging out the window counts as exercise. "Wanna take a load off?" Rob asked, offering Mr. Hurley a chair up on the porch, "How about an iced tea?" Mr. Hurley decided this might be a good midpoint in the evening's walk about.

You know he has been a fixture in this town for over thirty years. Carl says probably every woman in town has received a love letter from him. He's good-natured and quick with a kind word or a humorous story. When you ask him how he got his job he'll say, "Why, I stamped my foot," or he'll tell about some of his interesting encounters. A few years ago he returned a letter to one of the Birdie sisters, telling her it was too heavy and she needed to put more stamps on it. "Why," she asked, "will that make it lighter?"

Carl teases Mr. Hurley that "Old mail carriers don't die, they just lose their zip." But these days Mr. Hurley isn't laughing because he is worried about aging and his health.

Several months ago he noticed his food wasn't as tasty as it once was. In fact, nothing really tasted that good. He started noticing food in his refrigerator that had turned bad. But he only noticed it by color or texture. It finally dawned on him he'd lost his sense of smell.

Of course, he was careful to not let people know this, but it does create problems. You see, Mr. Hurley can never be sure of several of the things that used to not even give him pause. Is the milk bad, does he have a strong body odor, is the fish still fresh? Try as he might, he can't smell anything. To compensate, he's taken to using a wide variety of aftershaves and colognes. What is it Carl says, "The more per ounce, the better per-fume." Evidently, Mr. Hurley hasn't been wasting his money on fragrances.

And that exacerbates the problem. Now that he's using so much aftershave, no one can stand to get close to him. Of course, Mr. Hurley can tell people are avoiding him. And he assumes the reason is some bad smell. To cover it, he uses more cologne — it's a vicious cycle. Someone down at the Busy-Bee the other day wondered if the perfume samples put in magazines had so permeated Mr. Hurley's car that just by driving his route all day he absorbed the smell. Someone else said he was trying out a new brand: "Rankinsence."

Joan Lockwood came out on the porch and asked Mr. Hurley how he was enjoying the summer as she handed him his tea. "No complaints so far, I guess." Perhaps it was a flash of insight; perhaps it was Mr. Hurley's evening aftershave, deodorant, breath mint, hair tonic blend, or something else, but the subject turned to fragrances. Joan was trying to recall the lilac smell from their bushes, perhaps to cover in her own mind the amazing cocktail of fragrances that Mr. Hurley had concocted for that evening. Inquiring of Mr.

Hurley if he liked lilacs, she misspoke and asked if he enjoyed the smell of the roses. "I love roses, but sometimes they remind me of funerals. But yours smell great tonight."

But the Lockwoods' roses aren't in bloom. Joan suspected Mr. Hurley couldn't smell a thing. But just to test her hypothesis she took Mr. Hurley's glass and refilled it with tea and a dollop of vanilla extract.

"You make a good glass of iced tea, Joan," Mr. Hurley said, thanking her and taking a long swallow.

"Mr. Hurley, you don't have a sense of smell anymore, do you?" Joan stated more than asked.

"You don't need all of those scents you're wearing. Let me be your nose. I'll tell you if things are just right," she continued.

Rob sat there in the deepening dusk, amazed at Joan's detective skills. He had been hoping that all this was just a phase Mr. Hurley was going through. Of course, Rob explains everything with, "It's just a phase he's going through."

Actually, I'm a little disappointed. For a while I thought I was getting perfumed letters from an admirer. Even in your letters I had detected a slight citrus smell. When Carl heard all about this, he said, "And I thought Mr. Hurley was just trying to cover up the smell of dead letters."

We're all proud of you and all that's going on at your church. But remember, "Flattery is like perfume — a little goes a long way and should never be swallowed." Let me get this to the mailbox before Mr. Hurley gets here. We're praying for you and your church.

Love to all,
Elizabeth

Parts of a body
If the whole body were an eye, where would the hearing be? If the whole body were hearing, where would the sense of smell be? (1 Corinthians 12:17)

Dear Mike,

Well, church got out late on Sunday. I didn't get too much out of the last half of the sermon. Lately, it seems Reverend Answers' most interesting point is his stopping point. What is it Carl says? "Reverend Answers uses a gallon of words to express a spoonful of thought," which Sunday was how we've got to help our neighbor. But if the truth be known, I'd say most of us were distracted with the Olympics. You know, the town council worked out a lease agreement with the US Olympic committee to convert the old theater into a training site almost two years ago. The Olympic track team officials all thought our town would be perfect for training athletes. And, of course, the town was thrilled.

Of course, we were somewhat disappointed to learn that the team training here would be the Olympic race-walkers. Carl had several comments about how, "Some people walk to reduce and others being reduced to walking," and "Walking isn't a lost art; people still have to walk to the garage."

Well, they used the old theater as a weight training and aerobic center and the county roads as practice tracks. Mike, our disappointment has turned to outright joy at having them here. It never ceases to bring a smile to our faces when we come across one of them out on the roads. Talk about loose as a goose. Carl says they look like marionettes being operated by ferrets. We've tried to get behind them in their quest for the gold, although I don't think their chances are very good. We don't support it in the schools the way some countries do.

Carl went over to Lansing last Wednesday, to Reel Life, the video rental store that specializes in classics. On Friday night, he and Coralie invited a bunch of us over to view the 1966 classic *Walk, Don't Run* filmed at the 1964 Tokyo Olympics, which detailed American speed walker, Jim Hutton's quest for the Gold. Well, it isn't *Chariots of Fire* or *It Happened in Athens*, but it is inspiring. "It's a classic!" Carl said as the credits rolled. A matter of opinion, I suppose.

Saturday the video was due back at Reel Life, so Carl decided he'd run a few errands in town and then head over to Lansing. However, when he got to Lansing, somehow he'd been able to arrive without the video.

"This might not be so bad," Carl thought, "I'd like to own a copy of *Walk, Don't Run*. I must have left it in the Busy-Bee when I stopped for coffee this morning, I'll just buy it," he thought to himself.

"I was in here the other day to rent *Walk, Don't Run*," he began with the young clerk. "I'm afraid I've lost it, so, I'd like to pay for it," Carl explained.

"Let's see," said the clerk as he leafed through a price list. "Oh, yeah, here it is. That'll be $90."

"Ninety dollars!" Carl gasped in disbelief.

"Yes, sir, it's a classic," replied the clerk.

"So I've heard. Well, I'll try looking a little harder. See you later," Carl told him as he turned and left.

Carl retraced his steps to the Busy-Bee.

"Darlene, did I leave a video in here this morning?" Carl asked. "It was in a paper sack."

"I don't think so. But Rex cleaned up before he went home. He might have pitched it without even noticing, if it was in a paper bag."

So that's how it happened that Carl found himself in the alley behind the Busy-Bee. "Dipsy Dumpster," Carl mumbled to himself. "Now there's a definition of a collective noun." But one's own humor is seldom cheering. Carl was amazed at how much garbage could be generated by the Busy-Bee. He finally spied the bag in the far corner. Unfortunately, he had to climb in to fish it out.

As he was hopping in, Reverend Answers came driving down the alley. He often uses the alley as a shortcut to the library parking lot. Carl could only wave a hello as Reverend Answers drove past.

"Now that was strange," Reverend Answers thought to himself. "And did Carl look startled, no, not startled, but embarrassed. Chagrined, yes, that was it, chagrined."

201

He knew things were hard on Carl and Coralie since the paper closed. It didn't take Reverend Answers two minutes to figure that Carl was in the dumpster looking for food for him and Coralie. He could hardly believe his eyes, but there it was, irrefutable proof.

Carl was surprised when he returned from Lansing the second time Saturday after dropping off the video, to find an envelope addressed to him stuck in the door. He was more surprised to find six $20 bills and a note saying, "Your friends care about you."

The third time Carl came home from Lansing on Saturday he and Coralie had had a fine meal at The Portage House and purchased *Walk, Don't Run* from Reel Life Video.

"Well, this has been some kind of day. What do you say we invite the Answers over one night next week, and we'll all watch *Walk, Don't Run*. I know he'll find some good sermon material in it," Carl reasoned to Coralie.

Well, I'd better get this in the mail before Mr. Hurley, the mail carrier, gets here. We're praying for you and your church.

Love to all,
Elizabeth

Helping
So let us not grow weary in doing what is right, for we will reap at harvest time, if we do not give up. So then, whenever we have an opportunity, let us work for the good of all, and especially for those of the family of faith. (Galatians 6:9-10)

Dear Mike,

Well, church got out late on Sunday. I didn't get too much out of the last half of the sermon. Reverend Answers is either inimitable or illimitable. If the truth be known, my mind was kind of fixed on last week's county fair.

I guess you know how important the fair is for me. Why, this year I even agreed to help do some set-up for the 4-H displays. It was during that set-up time that I got acquainted with Scott. My guess is that you know someone like him. He's one of the "carneys" who travels with the midway shows from fairground to fairground. What is it Carl says? "They're grounds for a good time."

Well, maybe for some, but not everyone. I take my own trials in the pickle competition as but one example. I've tried everything possible to win a blue ribbon for my pickles, and every year that woman from Chapin takes home the prize. Actually, I had high hopes this year as I had modified my recipe.

Monday, I showed up with my pickles and a new lemon chiffon cake at the domestic arts building. After dropping things off for the judging I made my way to the 4-H barn. I was actually helping set up the sewing display area. Lugging tables around wasn't my idea of fun, so I tracked down one of the carneys on the midway, who happened to be Scott.

"Could you give me a hand with some tables?" I asked.

"I suppose so. What do you need?" he answered.

During the course of dragging the tables around we got fairly well acquainted.

"Where'd you get all those tattoos?" My curiosity got the better of me.

"Wichita, Clearwater, Norfolk, Wichita Falls, Abilene," he fired off in rapid succession as if reading a road map.

"I suppose there's a story for each one?" I asked gamely, straining under the weight of a table and the topic.

"No, mostly the same story. I drink too much," he answered.

"What about those numbers there on your arm?"

"Oh, that's my birth date," he said.

I studied the numbers for a minute. "Isn't that tomorrow?"

"Yes, I guess it is," he offered without much emotion.

"Well, are you going to celebrate?"

"Yeah, probably have a few drinks with some buddies in my trailer."

"No, let's do something else." I could hardly believe my own voice. "Let's have a birthday party right here."

And that's how it was that on Tuesday I baked another lemon chiffon cake. I assumed with the fair not officially open until Wednesday morning that we'd pretty well have the 4-H building to ourselves, save for the kids that were staying over with animals, or people stopping by at the last minute to drop off items for exhibit.

So I was fairly shocked when Scott showed up with about 25 or 30 people, all coworkers from the midway rides and the games-of-chance booths. Well, my chiffon cake was gone in a minute. What the heck, I thought, I don't need another cake blue ribbon. I'll go get my first cake from the domestic arts building. Carl says, "If you want to have your cake and eat it, too, you'd better bake two cakes." But tonight that may not be enough, I thought. The second of my cakes was soon gone, too. But in the meantime, another cake had mysteriously appeared, and then another, as had an additional 20 or 25 people who were curious as to what was going on: more carneys and more food. And once aware it was a party, they just stayed. Another cake, then another. I dreaded to think where all those cakes were coming from. Even though I knew.

"Here, try one of these. They're delicious!" I heard someone say.

Can you imagine my surprise when I turned to see my almost prize-winning pickles being passed around.

"I never tasted better," came another voice.

And just that fast, the pickles were gone; then the cakes, and finally, the people, leaving just Scott and me.

I went back over to the cake display table, not a single cake left. The table had been virtually picked clean. The pickle table fared some better: only one or two pints missing as near as I could

204

tell. The Chapin woman's jar had been passed over. Who says you can't tell by looking!

I walked back over to the 4-H building to find Scott still there. He had a look of absolute bliss.

"Man, I didn't know I had so many friends," he said.

I wondered if this was the right time or not for a little tough love. After all, I think it was the cakes who had the friends.

"I'm glad you had a good time," I honestly replied. "I did, too."

"I appreciate what you did. You know sometimes I feel like people are divided into good and bad, and it's the good who do the dividing."

I was somewhat embarrassed by the truth of his comment.

"You know what our motto on the midway is?" Scott asked and then answered before I could say, "No." " 'None but the brave deserves the fair.' Thanks for being brave. I think I'll remember this as long as I live."

I wondered how he knew the quote was from Dryden's *Alexander's Feast* and I responded with a line from Shakespeare's *Measure for Measure*, "The hand that hath made you fair, hath made you good."

Well, I'd better get this in the mail before Mr. Hurley, the mail carrier, gets here. We're praying for you and your congregation.

Love to all,
Elizabeth

Judging others
My brothers and sisters, do you with your acts of favoritism really believe in our glorious Lord Jesus Christ? For if a person with gold rings and in fine clothes comes into your assembly, and if a poor person in dirty clothes also comes in, and if you take notice of the one wearing the fine clothes and say, "Have a seat here, please," while to the one who is poor you say, "Stand there," or, "Sit at my feet," have you not made distinctions among yourselves, and become judges with evil thoughts? (James 2:1-4)

Dear Mike,

Well, church got out late on Sunday. I didn't get too much out of the last half of the sermon. Carl said, "It's always dullest just before yawn," and "You can't get your ears pierced at church, but you can at least get them bored."

Well, it's been anything but boring around here lately, and, frankly, my hands hurt like the dickens. I don't know where to begin with all that's happened in the last couple of months. I guess it all started with a report in the Lansing paper listing Maybe as a bedroom community. You know, for a lot of us, "bedroom" isn't a word we use in polite conversation. So you can imagine how much we like the thought of being associated with the bedroom. We prefer to think of ourselves as a kitchen community or a parlor community, even a mudroom community. The gist of the article was that Great Lake State Cable View was considering expanding into surrounding bedroom communities and listing us as one such place.

As I said, that was a couple months ago, but that has been all people have been talking about down at the Busy-Bee Café. I heard Carl say, "Bedroom community sounds like a lot of bunk to me." You know I've always thought "early to bed, early to rise" makes one a farmer. But there are more and more people building out here who don't farm. I'd still contend that no civilized person would go to bed the same day they plan to get up. I must admit some of the new people out on Scenic Lake do seem to keep irregular hours.

Of course, most of the talk at the Busy-Bee wasn't wasted on bedrooms or sleeping schedules but on whether or not we wanted cable television.

You'd be surprised at what strong opinions are held on this. Why, the town was just about divided down the middle after the "That's One Man's Opinion" that Parnell gave on WOPE Radio.

The radio station has come out firmly against this infringement upon what they see as their responsibility to fulfill their mission of

"bringing the world of today and tomorrow into your kitchen."
(Whether or not Parnell and Wally have actually succeeded on that
motto is open to discussion.) Some suggest they have been much
more successful in teaching the truth, that "silence is golden."

You may recall that WOPE Radio is only licensed to broadcast during daylight hours, which almost precludes the possibility
of "bringing today or tomorrow" into anyone's bedroom.

Parnell's opinion editorial cited the threat to morals that cable
offered, the lack of local control, the fact that our hard-earned
money would flow out of town, and his final trump card, that it
was downright un-biblical, misquoting Judges: "And Samson said
unto Delilah, 'If they bind me with new cables that were never
before used, then I shall be weak, and as any other man' " (Judges
16:11).

Well, there you have it in a nutshell, people divided along pre-
dictable lines, with WOPE Radio editorials each morning only
adding fuel to the fire. As usual, this debate fueled considerably
more heat than light.

Light was what was indeed needed on a Thursday last month.
We were all in the dark. That was the day the electricity went off
all over town. Here a couple months later, I think the Consumer's
Power people have finally traced the problem to the Busy-Bee
Café. Evidently, Rex had purchased a couple of "Cyclonic Cook-
ers" that were some sort of oven that offered the speed of a micro-
wave and the browning ability of a conventional oven. Speed has
its price; in this case that was increased electricity use. Unfortunately, when Rex plugged them both in and fired them up, fuses
started blowing. First the Reynolds' building went, then the poles
out back, then the transformer at Main and Oak, and then township substation, then Lansing, then Detroit, then Ohio, then parts
of Canada, and the eastern United States; at least that's the way
the investigators have reconstructed it.

By Friday it was clear that the power companies were having
trouble getting the power back on. Of course, Parnell and the others at WOPE Radio were quick to point out how much we all need
radio and how unreliable television is.

On Friday, people were still in pretty good spirits about the outage. I ate all the ice cream in my freezer to prevent throwing it out, which I dare say will put anyone in good spirits.

Carl was joking, "The future of electricity depends upon current matters." WOPE Radio gave hourly news updates and probably had its highest Arbitron ratings ever.

But Saturday, Parnell broadcasted an urgent help plea for the Simmons' dairy farm. It seemed their diesel generators had been overtaxed and couldn't produce enough power to run the milking machines any longer. The Simmons milk about 450 head, so they'd asked for neighbors to come lend a hand, so to speak.

When I got out there at about 9:30 there were cars parked from the barn all the way out to the road and off on the shoulder.

Carl was in rare form, directing traffic and offering advice to people as they arrived. "Cows don't give milk. You have to take it," and "Want to know how long cows should be milked? — same as short ones!" "Be careful out there, you can hear cowbells, but not cow horns." We all felt relieved he didn't drag out his "udderly ridiculous" stuff.

"One sure way to keep milk from souring is to leave it in the cow," he'd say every now and again. Well, that might be true, but it was souring the cows; you could tell from their lowing that their discomfort was considerable.

I'd guess it had been thirty years since I'd last had a cow in the stanchions with a milk pail underneath. But some skills are not soon forgotten. Of course, for the young people who came out it was a chance to learn milking first hand, so to speak.

I was amazed at the number of new people I met out there Saturday. I bet half of the people were recent "bedroom" immigrants from Lansing.

Nothing like an emergency to bring people together; by Sunday most of the arguing over the merits of cable had stopped.

As I recall, I'd heard Carl say there are three ways to get something done: Do it yourself, hire it done, or forbid a teenager to do it. But there is obviously a fourth — ask your neighbors to lend a hand, speaking of which, now you know why my hands were sore Sunday.

I'd better get this in the mail before Mr. Hurley, the mail carrier, gets here. We're praying for you and your congregation.

Love to all,
Elizabeth

Helping
Bear one another's burdens, and in this way you will fulfill the law of Christ. (Galatians 6:2)

Clock Off
November 4

Dear Mike,

Well, church got out late on Sunday. I didn't get too much out of the last half of the sermon. Reverend Answers had what Carl calls a measured message: thought by the inch, delivered by the foot. We were held *spiel*bound. It just seems like everything is running late these days. I kept trying to glance over my shoulder to the clock at the back of the sanctuary just to make sure my watch hadn't stopped. George Wilson was trying to gauge whether or not the clock on his and Bertha's bedstead had stopped.

Time has been on everybody's mind around here lately. Carl says we can all take a lesson from the clock, "The best way to pass time is to keep one's hands busy." We start noticing the days getting shorter as summer loosens its grip.

As Carl says, "Time waits for no man, but it does stand still for women over 38." But even that's not true, as the Wilsons can tell. Bertha's sister in Indiana is seriously ill and not expected to live more than a few more weeks. Her health has been failing for over a year. So Friday, John and Cheryl drove Bertha down to Indiana. Twice Bertha asked John, "How much longer?" even though she knew fairly well the distance to go.

"You're sounding like Mike," Cheryl chided, remembering how he was the most impatient one on trips.

"I wonder if we should have left Mike home alone?" she asked John and Bertha. She was keenly aware of Mike's disappointment at having to stay with his grandfather, George.

"I'm old enough to stay here by myself; Matt got to when he was a senior," Mike had whined.

"It isn't you, your grandfather needs someone to stay with him," she responded, which was true. But she thought to herself, *When we left Matt and you here, Matt didn't have a girlfriend, and he did have a younger brother who would snitch.* "You and Grandpa can help each other out. Really, he needs you. Your grandmother will rest easier knowing you're there," she said.

You may recall when I wrote that Mike and Kaitlyn Eston were seeing each other. I'd say their relationship is developing nicely. They date regularly, talk on the phone often, and if that weren't enough, they have instant messages for late night communication.

"Your mother tells me your curfew is midnight," George told Mike as he was heading out the door to Kaitlyn's on Friday night.

If time was going slowly for the three occupants of John's car, it fairly flew by for the two occupants of Mike's car as they talked in Kaitlyn's driveway after their date. In fact, Mike was shocked to realize it was 12:45 and he'd promised to be home at 12:00. Thankfully, George was asleep when Mike got home at 1:00.

What is it Carl says? "Love is like a photograph; it develops in the dark." Mike had enjoyed the evening in Kaitlyn's company and fell asleep looking forward to her company again Saturday night.

As he waited to go to her house, he couldn't believe how slow time went when he was waiting to get together and how quickly it passed once they were together.

George had suspected Mike hadn't gotten home before curfew Friday night, but as he was sound asleep he couldn't be sure. Nevertheless, there was some evasiveness in Mike's answers to George's questions about the previous night.

"You'll be home by midnight tonight, right?" George questioned.

"That's the curfew," Mike replied cheerily, but avoiding a straight answer.

"What about you, Grandpa? When is your curfew?"

"On Saturday it's 9:00, right after Lawrence Welk," George answered. "Do me a favor," he continued, "wake me up when you get home, just so I know you're safe."

So at 1:15 Mike was quietly entering his grandfather's bedroom. His plan was to say he was home without mentioning the time. Just as he was about to speak, his eye lit on the brightest light in the room, the clock radio with the illuminated numbers showing all too clearly the time as 1:17.

"I'll fix that," Mike thought to himself as he whisked the clock off the nightstand and quickly reset it for 12:07.

211

"Grandpa, I'm home," he said rousing George.

"What time is it?" George asked groggily.

"It looks like it's just after 12:00," Mike said indicating the clock. Now the perfect crime would have had Mike slipping back in and resetting the clock. But this isn't a perfect world. Mike went back after about thirty minutes to add the deleted hour. But in trying to keep one eye on his grandfather and the other on the clock, he added two hours.

Carl says a clock enables a person to rise in the world. It did George, exactly one hour and ten minutes early. Mike was still sound asleep when George rolled over and looked to see it was 7:20.

Well, a man who starts the day with an hour and ten minute head start is going to arrive places ahead of time. And that was the case when George arrived at church at ten 'til nine for the homebuilders Sunday school class. He was surprised to be the first there. In fact, it was the first time in forty years he was the first to arrive. As a rule, George and Bertha arrive about five minutes late.

"I wonder if Ma's been holding me back all these years?" George thought to himself. "It is strange that no one is here; is this Sunday?" he continued, trying to make sense of a locked up church. "Well, I'll just go next door to the parsonage and see if Reverend Answers knows why no one is here," George decided.

"Come in, George," Reverend Answers said, rather surprised to find one of the parishioners on the parsonage porch. "What brings you by so early?" he continued.

"What brings me by?" George thought but said, "Why isn't anyone at church?"

"Well, Sunday school doesn't start for another hour," Reverend Answers replied, wondering if perhaps George had had a ministroke or TIA or something similar.

"Not for an hour?" George asked. "What time is it?"

"Just 8:15," Reverend Answers replied. "You want to wait in here or shall I open the church for you?"

George looked at his watch, as Reverend Answers did, and saw it was 8:15.

"Well, I must have read my clock on the bedstead at home wrong," George concluded. "I'll go over to the church and wait." George was learning just how slow time goes when you're waiting. But finally some people started to arrive.

Carl was very surprised to see George already there for Sunday school. He said. "The man who is early of late, used to be behind before and now is first, at last" (or words to that effect). All of which helped George feel better. But by the end of worship, which got out late, the mood had passed.

Well, I'd better get this in the mail before Mr. Hurley, the mail carrier, gets here. We're praying for you and your congregation.

Love to all,
Elizabeth

Time
And the sun stood still, and the moon stopped, until the nation took vengeance on their enemies. Is this not written in the Book of Jashar? The sun stopped in midheaven, and did not hurry to set for about a whole day. (Joshua 10:13)

Dear Mike,

Well, church got out late on Sunday. I didn't get too much out of the last half of the sermon. Actually, I loved the sermon except for two things: my ears. Carl says, "It was a skyscraper sermon, lots of stories and not much in between."

Lately, Reverend Answers has been preaching about sin. He said there are 728 sins noted in the Bible. I guess more than a few people wanted a look at the list to see if they'd missed out on anything. I'd say Reverend Answers can let up on the sin sermons for a while. Holiday shopping has made most of us too poor to afford much of it.

I stopped by the Busy-Bee Café yesterday, which was something of an ordeal as the roads and walks were quite icy. Carl was telling everyone how he'd lost his balance. "It always happens when Coralie goes shopping this time of year." Someone else said his family had brought back from the mall everything but prosperity. The general agreement was to shop early if not often.

I don't know, I seem to enjoy catalogue and online shopping more with each passing year. Maybe it's because I'm getting older, or maybe it's because I don't like the crowds, but if the truth be told I think I enjoy having Mr. Hurley, the mail carrier, come up to the house to deliver the parcels. He's always a bringer of good news, even if it isn't in the mail.

I guess when Carl says, "This is the time of year when people don't think of the past or future, but focus on the present," he's right. "Present makes the heart grow fonder," is one of his quotes.

Well, not everyone is able to get their mind off the past. Blaine has been upset with his niece and nephew since last January. Why didn't his youngest brother Chris and sister-in-law teach those kids to write thank-you notes? At Blaine's house they have rules. You don't use the gift until the thank-you note is written.

And last Christmas, Blaine and his family were struggling financially, something Chris' family seems immune to. Of course, living in the Chicago area might be considered as something of struggle, if you ask Blaine.

Well, one thing's for sure in Blaine's mind: this year Amanda and Mark aren't getting anything from Blaine (and maybe not Chris and Dru, as far as that goes).

Blaine wasn't in the best of moods when Carolyn sent him up into the attic to get out the Christmas decorations. But he spent the Friday after Thanksgiving dutifully hauling down boxes, stringing lights, and assembling the tree.

I guess it was on about the fifth trip to the attic that Blaine noticed two packages still wrapped in brown paper. You can imagine his shock as he turned over the first to see his nephew's name and address, and the second had his niece's name and address on it.

Blaine sat right down on the floor looking at the boxes. "Well, this explains a lot," he thought to himself. "Might not be fair to expect someone to write a 'thank-you' note for a gift they never received."

"I wonder if I could mail them for this year? It would save a little," he continued to muse.

Then he realized even though he'd purchased the gifts, for the life of him, he couldn't remember what he'd gotten them. He thought it was something to wear. If it was, he reasoned the kids might have outgrown them. He just stared at the boxes.

"Well, I've got to look inside," he said aloud. Carolyn was at the foot of the stairs ready to come up to see what was keeping Blaine.

"Look inside for what?" she hollered up the stairs.

Brought back to reality, Blaine said, "Nothing, just talking to myself. I'll be right down." Then he mumbled to himself, "Look inside myself would be the correct answer."

"I'm going to run over to Lansing to the mall this afternoon," he announced to Carolyn when he descended the stairs.

"What on earth for! You hate to shop. This has got to be one of the busiest shopping days of the year," she replied.

"I need to get something for Amanda and Mark."

"I thought they were off the gift list and onto the you-know-what list."

When Blaine got to the mall, he was feeling so guilty he really splurged on the kids. In fact, he really put some time and thought in each of the kid's gifts. Now all he has to do is figure out what to do with the two sweatshirts that say "It's Cool in the Refrigerator Magnet Museum," with Magnet Museum in much smaller type.

Well, I'd better get this in the mail before Mr. Hurley, the mail carrier, gets here. Who knows, he might even have to stop at the house today. We're praying for you and your congregation.

Love to all,
Elizabeth

Gratitude
And let the peace of Christ rule in your hearts, to which indeed you were called in the one body. And be thankful. (Colossians 3:15)

Christmas Cookies
December 28

Dear Mike,

Well, church got out late on Sunday. I didn't get too much out of the last half of the sermon. Our attendance was off somewhat last Sunday what with it being Christmas Day. I asked Carl if he had missed church the previous week. "No, not a bit," he said. I think Reverend Answers believes the art of preaching is to take a two-minute idea and dilute it with a twenty-minute vocabulary. It seems to me that the best ingredient to add to a sermon is shortening.

Speaking of shortening, I went through my fair share of it baking for Christmas. What is it Carl says? "A baker is one who kneads much and then gives away what she kneads."

I know they're the subject of countless jokes, but I made about a dozen fruitcakes this year. I always ask Carl if he knows, "What's the best thing to put in a fruitcake?" When he says he doesn't know, I say, "Your teeth!" But actually, I think the secret to my fruitcakes is the bourbon I soak them in.

Making as many cakes as I do, I'm always on the lookout for a sale on bourbon. So I usually buy it in Lansing at the Super Val-U-Mart. Anyway, I'm not sure everyone here knows what I need the bourbon for, and I do have my reputation to consider.

In fact, I've been doing most of my shopping over there, lately. The prices are better than here at Bradley's. I'll admit it isn't always easy shopping at the warehouse store, though. I mean it takes me thirty minutes to find the instant coffee. And I always spend more than I expect to. It's what Carl refers to as "the high-cost-of-leaving." Oh well, I always wanted to spend money lavishly. I just never expected it to be on food.

The Monday before Christmas, I was working on some Christmas cookies for the carolers. I'd made nutmeg logs, which had just about depleted all the nutmeg I had on hand. I thought I might make some pfefferneusse, which calls for sizable amounts of nutmeg. I also noticed I was out of baking powder.

I decided I'd run into town to Bradley's Market and pick up the spices, baking powder, and a few other things.

Spring I like and summer and fall, too, but winter leaves me cold. So I suppose I wasn't in the best of spirits when I reached the store. Can you imagine my surprise when at 9:40 a.m. it wasn't open! A sign on the door announced the new hours, 10:00-8:00.

I wondered when the hours had changed. I tried to think of the last time I had shopped there in the morning, or the last time I was in there at all. It must have been two months or more; I couldn't believe it.

I headed up to the Busy-Bee Café to have a cup of coffee while I waited for Bradley's to open. Darlene always gets the place decorated so nice for Christmas. She says, "Well, I spend more time here than at home." She does go a bit overboard. Carl says you don't know if she's celebrating the birth of Jesus or Consumers' Power.

I was back at Bradley's a couple minutes after 10:00.

"When did you change your hours?" I asked.

"Just before Thanksgiving," Walt replied.

Actually, I was noticing some other changes. The store was completely rearranged.

"Where are the spices?"

"Over by the flowers."

"Flowers?" I wondered.

"Where's the baking powder?"

"Don't carry it anymore," Walt answered.

"You don't carry Clabber Girl?" I asked in disbelief.

"No, there just wasn't any demand for it. I probably sold three or four cans a year. Now it's just meats and specialty items. We're carving out a country kitchen niche market."

I couldn't believe my ears. "Niche, niche, niche," I mumbled to myself.

"Too many people are taking their business to the Super Val-U-Mart." Walt continued, "I can't compete, so I had to change."

"Do you still carry flour?" I questioned.

"Only stone ground whole wheat."

"Sugar?"

"Only Hawaiian unrefined."

218

"Coffee?"

"Only Colombian High Mountain."

"Bour—" I stopped before putting bourbon near the top of my shopping list. "Nutmeg?"

"The finest New Guinea has to offer."

"I'll take it."

"Do you want me to grind it here or will you grind it at home?"

"You're kidding, right?"

He wasn't.

"Give me a pound of coffee, too, and I'll try five pounds of that sugar."

Actually, it was a pleasant experience. I had a cup of eggnog (brown eggs, I guess) and browsed while Walt went about the store filling my order.

I felt sort of guilty as I drove home. I mean if I'd kept shopping Bradley's rather than the warehouse store, he'd still be carrying Clabber Girl, which, by the way, I was able to borrow from Coralie, who'd bought the 32-oz. canister some time ago and doesn't expect to use it up in this lifetime.

The next day I took a break for some pfefferneusse and coffee. The coffee was superb and the cookies the best I've ever made. I wrapped up a small box and took them back to Bradley's. I was surprised to see several people shopping. Of course, it was late afternoon.

"Here, put these out as a sample of how good your New Guinea nutmeg is," I said, handing him the box.

"Thanks. By the way, you might want to check out the other spices. I've just put out some new items," he said with a knowing wink.

Sure enough, there between the anise seeds from Italy and the bay leaves from Jamaica sat the small white Clabber Girl canister with the bright red letters, and seeing that girl with the plate full of biscuits walking away from the kitchen was like bumping into an old friend.

Now if you look closely it appears the girl's brother is blowing bubbles in the background, to the delight of the youngest sister and the family kitten.

You know it doesn't take much baking powder, just a pinch or two but without it you can't use sour cream or buttermilk. It takes away the sourness and it lightens everything.

"Merry Christmas," Walt said, handing me the baking powder.

"Merry Christmas yourself," I said with a real note of Christmas cheer.

Well, I'd better get this in the mail before Mr. Hurley, the mail carrier, gets here. We're praying for you and your congregation.

Love to all,
Elizabeth

Leavening/Transformation
He told them another parable: "The kingdom of heaven is like yeast that a woman took and mixed in with three measures of flour until all of it was leavened." (Matthew 13:33)

And all of us, with unveiled faces, seeing the glory of the Lord as though reflected in a mirror, are being transformed into the same image from one degree of glory to another; for this comes from the Lord, the Spirit. (2 Corinthians 3:18)

Scripture Index

Topical Index

CPSIA information can be obtained at www.ICGtesting.com
Printed in the USA
LVOW131411081012

301976LV00004B/19/P